SUCCESSFUL

HUMAN RELATIONS

SUCCESSFUL
HUMAN RELATIONS

Principles and Practice in Business,
in the Home, in Government

by William J. Reilly, Ph.D.

Business Consultant; Founder and Director,
National Institute for Straight Thinking;

Author of
"The Twelve Rules for Straight Thinking"
"The Law of Intelligent Action"
"How to Avoid Work"

HARPER & BROTHERS, PUBLISHERS, NEW YORK

Library of Congress catalog card number: 52-6280

This book
is affectionately dedicated
to the memory of

"KING GEORGE" FOLLOWS

MASTER IN HUMAN RELATIONS AND HEAD
OF THE COMMERCIAL ENGINEERING DE-
PARTMENT AT CARNEGIE INSTITUTE OF
TECHNOLOGY, FOR IT WAS HE WHO FIRST
INTERESTED ME IN HUMAN ENGINEERING

CONTENTS

PREFACE

The history of whatever progress man has made to date is a story of his adaptation to the laws of his environment. Those who abide by these laws usually grow and prosper; those who fail to do so are likely to have a rather unhappy time of it.

One of the jobs of science is to summarize our experience and to formulate our knowledge of our environment into simple rules, laws, and principles that can be easily understood, consciously applied, and readily communicated for the purpose of improving our everyday lives.

During the past twenty years, at the National Institute for Straight Thinking, some progress has been made in developing such fundamental concepts in three main areas:

1. *The Twelve Rules For Straight Thinking* have been defined and a book under this title has been published which shows how the rules can be applied to business and personal problems.

2. *The Law of Intelligent Action* has been defined and a book under this title applies the law to business relations.

3. Now, in this book, *The Principles of Successful Human Relations* are defined and applied in business, in the home, and in government. Portions of the material found in this book were originally published in an earlier book titled *How to Improve Your Human Relations.*

Meanwhile, the rules for straight thinking, the law of

intelligent action, and the principles of successful human relations have also been applied to career problems in the popular book *How to Avoid Work,* which shows you how to get into a job you really enjoy and how to plan the various stages of your life.

The development of the fundamental concepts found in this book and in the other books mentioned has an interesting background, and those who would like to read the story are referred to the Appendix.

This book has been written for businessmen, parents, government workers, educators, students, or anyone else who is interested in the fundamental principles of successful human relations. It is used as the basic text in human relations at the National Institute for Straight Thinking and can be used either as a textbook or a reference book wherever formal courses of study in human relations are offered at the college or adult level.

Grateful acknowledgment is hereby given to the many business and industrial clients and the members and alumni of the National Institute for Straight Thinking, far too numerous to mention, who contributed most of the factual case material upon which this book is based.

The presentation of the material in this book has been greatly clarified by the continued editorial criticism given by Gladys Bogue Reilly.

March, 1952   W. J. R.

SUCCESSFUL

HUMAN RELATIONS

CHAPTER I

Introduction

There are only two ways in which you can get anyone to do what you want him to do: one is by persuasion; the other by force.

The more intelligent we become, the more we are inclined to employ the use of persuasion and to abandon the use of force in our relations with others.

And yet, if we are to avoid a limited and unrealistic view of the simple problems in human relations which you and I face on our jobs, in our homes, and in our local or national or world attempts at law and order, we must admit that, try as we might to use persuasion, there are many cases in which persuasion may fail and there is nothing left for us to do except to run away, surrender, or use force.

In raising and educating our children, some kind of discipline may be necessary when persuasion fails. And whenever we reluctantly impose our will on a child, we always hope that, later on, the child will see that what we have done was for his own good.

In a world that has not yet come of age, we see adults, in their blind pursuit of some prized objective, selfishly follow a course of action which threatens other people with loss or damage or destruction. If someone tries to undermine your reputation, or your job, or your company, or your marriage, or your home; if a thief tries to rob you; or if an international aggressor tries to take over your country, you may

1

want seriously to consider the possibility of using whatever force is at your command. You may want to "give him the works" first and then try to make a convert out of him later on.

In short, there are cases in which you may elect not to run away and not to surrender, but to use force and wait until after the smoke of battle clears away before you try to persuade an opponent that you have acted in his best interests.

The main trouble, however, is that we are likely to use force when it is not justified. When we are *right* and we *know* it, and when we are *strong enough* to overpower the other fellow, it is so easy to turn bully and to use force—even when there is plenty of time for persuasion.

Because of this flagrant misuse of force, many people with mature minds would like to see the use of force in human relations completely eliminated. They contend properly that force is a dangerous instrument at best, and that, in the last analysis, the only way any human difference or conflict can ever be settled, and a common agreement arrived at which even approaches a mutual satisfaction, is through peaceful persuasion. These people feel that force is futile in human relations, that it is the opposite of persuasion, that you must think in terms of either one or the other, that one is incompatible with the other, that you cannot reconcile the two.

No wonder there is so much confusion concerning how we ought to go about solving our everyday problems in human relations. We see this confusion in all kinds of human situations.

Parents argue about whether children should ever be spanked, and if so, when. Many are at a loss to know what to do when Junior refuses to eat his dinner.

Educators engage in heated discussions about whether

children should be kept in line by discipline or be given a free rein to express themselves in their own ways.

Young men and women, eager to get ahead careerwise, come out of our schools with an insufficient awareness of the importance of sound human relations in achieving their career objectives, and seem bewildered as to just how they should go about landing the job they really want and getting a raise or a promotion or any other kind of favorable recognition in their chosen field.

The divorce rate is up, largely because there are so many husbands and wives who have no predetermined plan for settling their differences—large or small.

Business leaders have been agreeing for a long time that the success of any top executive, junior executive, foreman, or supervisor depends primarily on his "ability to handle people." But business organizations have been slow to install training programs designed to develop this required ability, with the result that employers, executives, foremen, and supervisors commonly make inexcusable errors in handling individual employees and union groups. They are still inclined to act as wavering opportunists, dealing with similar cases in different ways on different days, depending on how they feel at the moment, simply because they have not developed any specific operating procedures and personal skills that are based on a thorough understanding of human nature.

And, as America grows in power and influence, there is anything but a meeting of the minds on how we should respond to the threat of international aggressors who would destroy our way of life—some contending that military power is the only thing that counts in our time; others that what we are really involved in is a struggle for the minds of men and that we must spend more money on that and not waste our funds on economic or military expenditures.

Obviously, we shall continue to have arguments about the use of persuasion and the use of force, we shall continue to be confused concerning the solution of our everyday human problems at home and abroad, and we shall continue to make expensive mistakes until we begin to pay more attention to the fundamental laws of human behavior.

There are three good reasons why man has been slow in discovering exactly what these laws are.

In the first place, if we review the long history of man, we find that he has acted much like an ape for quite a stretch— millions of years, in fact—and that the business of acting like a gentleman is a comparatively new idea with him. He's bought himself some nice clothes and covered himself with a thin veneer of "civilization." And, in recent years, he has made phenomenal progress in applying scientific methods to the material things outside himself. He can produce gases, germs, and bombs, with which he can even destroy himself. But he is just now getting around to the business of exploring the operations of the one little organ inside his head that dictates everything he does.

And this is understandable.

When man lived in small family or tribal groups, his main problem was to adapt himself to his *physical* environment—to secure food, shelter, clothing, and to protect himself from the elements and his natural enemies. But now we have discovered many of the laws which govern our physical and material environment. We have gone a long way toward conquering our physical and material environment. Consequently, we have multiplied and grouped ourselves into states and nations with ever closer ties of communication and trade, with the result that our main problem now is to learn how to live together—how to adapt ourselves to our complex *human* environment.

The second big reason why we have been slow in discovering the basic principles of successful human relations is that, when we violate one of the laws of human behavior, there is usually a delayed reaction involved. We may offend a person or take an unfair advantage of him without suffering any obvious penalty for years. Even then we may not associate the penalty with the mistake. In fact, we need never admit such mistakes. We can always rationalize what we have done as being justified under the circumstances.

Not so in our material world. The penalties for violating these laws are usually much swifter. We all know that if we defy the law of gravity and jump out of a tenth-floor window, it is almost certain to upset our entire day. If our factory is not built in accordance with the physical laws which govern a sound structure, we soon know it; if our machines are overloaded, they quickly fail; if a law of chemistry is ignored, there may be a violent explosion.

Because the penalty is so often delayed when we violate a law in human relations, we are actually unaware of many of the mistakes we make. And because we are so ingenious in rationalizing the mistakes we *are* aware of—satisfying ourselves that we did the right thing under the circumstances or blaming our mistakes on other people or on circumstances beyond our control—we are able to go to sleep at night with the general satisfaction that other people may be crazy but we're all right.

And that leads us to the third and perhaps the most important reason why man has been slow to improve his relations with others.

Man is an egotistical animal. He'll do almost anything to save face and to prove that he's right, even when he has the sneaking feeling that he's wrong about the whole thing.

He has found out that he cannot successfully argue with the laws of the moon or the sun or the stars or of his immediate physical environment. But he still finds considerable room for his egotistical opinions on the playground of human relations.

Although we may recognize that we are living in a world ruled more by emotion than by reason, and although we can often see that others are unwise or unfair in their dealings with people, each of us is inclined to feel that in *his own* relations with others, his judgments are sound and generous and he's pretty much of a lovable character.

Many of us who would not think of offering advice on problems which involve the laws of chemistry or physics speak up freely when it comes to problems which involve the laws of human relations. Nearly everyone thinks he is a good judge of people. We are our own psychologist and social science expert, ready to view almost any human problem through our own eyes, rather than objectively, and ready to pass our own personal judgment on the strengths or weaknesses of people and to predict how they will or should behave under circumstances that we know little about.

Handicapped by these comfortable delusions of egotism and self-satisfaction, we have been slow indeed to study the facts of human relations, to remove our own personal opinions, to clear the air of confusion, and to recognize the scientific principles which can safely be used to reduce our mistakes and to improve our batting average in solving the everyday human problems of life.

We might as well recognize, for our own good, that there are unchanging and everlasting laws which govern human behavior just as there are immutable laws which govern the character of all material things. The sooner we realize that we cannot violate any of these human laws without suffering, any more than we can defy the law of gravity without getting hurt, the sooner we will begin to exercise the same care in the solution of human problems as we have in the solution of material problems, to reduce "man's inhumanity to man," and to enjoy more of the rewards of successful human relations in our work, in our home, in our community, in our nation, and in all our international relations.

And man is capable of all this. For, in spite of his shortcomings, man has a lot to recommend him. He has proved over and over again that he has a brain capable of reason when his survival is threatened or when his desires to improve himself are stimulated. And man has proved over and over again that he has a heart with certain spiritual qualities that often inspire him to magnificent expressions of self-sacrifice and human service.

It's going to take a lot of patient teaching in our classrooms and in our homes and in the places where we work, but as soon as man is shown, by simple example, that it really pays him in material rewards and in spiritual satisfaction to abide by the laws of human nature, he'll make fewer mistakes, lose much of his short-sightedness, and become more interested in serving others.

In the following chapters, we shall proceed with our exploration of the fundamental principles of successful human relations and how they can be profitably applied to your everyday human problems.

We shall define the four mental levels in all human relations and we shall find out how the principles of persuasion can be used to open closed minds, win the confidence of others, and inspire their belief. We shall see what place force has in our human relations and we shall determine the three basic conditions under which we may consider the use of force with some degree of safety, at home or abroad.

CHAPTER II

The Four Mental Levels
in All Human Relations

If everyone you knew, everyone you met, believed everything you said, you could have just about anything you
wanted.

The trouble is that most people's minds are closed, so
much of the time, to the things you suggest.

You may not have thought of it in just this way, but
actually you are on one of four mental levels with every
person you know.

MENTAL LEVEL NO. 1—*The Closed Mind*

This is the "doghouse" level in which people think "Nuts
to you" or "Oh yeah?"

No matter what you say, they're "agin" it. Their minds
are closed to anything you suggest. Can you think of anyone
like that?

MENTAL LEVEL NO. 2—*The Open Mind*

This is the "show me" level in which people say "What
makes you think so?" These people will *listen* to what you
have to say, but you've got to give them plenty of evidence,
you've got to prove your point forty ways from Sunday before they'll do what you say.

MENTAL LEVEL NO. 3—*Confidence*

These people have confidence in you. Their attitude toward you is cooperative and friendly. They are willing to do what you want, but they want to know the main reasons why, and these reasons have to "make sense."

MENTAL LEVEL NO. 4—*Belief*

This is the "anything you say is o.k. by me" level. These people do what you ask without question. They need no evidence, no proof. They *believe* in you.

No matter what the situation is, it makes a whale of a difference—this mental level business.

For example, when an overworked husband arrives home at 2 A.M. after a long hard day and night at the office, anything can happen—depending on where he stands with his wife.

Let's follow him home and see.

The front door closes quietly and opens his wife's other eye. She calls downstairs, "Is that you, Henry?"

"Yes, dear," he replies wearily.

"Where have you been?" she asks. (She's at his side now, roping her negligee.)

"Working late at the office, dear," he explains.

"Oh, then you must be tired, darling," smiles the little wife, sympathetically. "Don't you want something to eat before you go to bed?"

Now *there's* a *belief* relationship!

Suppose, however, the conversation runs like this:

Henry enters the front door. His wife calls downstairs, "Is that you, Henry?"

"Yes, dear," he replies wearily.

"Where have *you* been?" (She's at his side now, roping her negligee, a puzzled look in her eyes.)

"Working late at the office, dear," he explains.

"Working at the office until this time of night? Must have been a mighty important job!"

"It *was,* dear," says Henry, reaching into his pocket. "Here's a wire that came from the Chicago office insisting that we finish our reports before tomorrow."

"Well, I think they're working you too hard at that old office, darling. They ought to be paying you more money," comments the little wife. "Do you want something to eat before you go to bed?"

Now there's a *confidence* relationship! High confidence!

Suppose, however, the conversation runs something like this:

Enter Henry. His wife calls downstairs.

"Is that you, Henry?"

"Yes, dear," he replies wearily.

"Where have *you* been?" she demands. (She's at his side now, roping her negligee. But there's a penetrating, quizzical look about her narrowed eyes.)

"Working late at the office, dear," he explains.

"Working at the office till this time of night?" she asks, doubtingly. "Must have been a mighty important job!"

"It was, dear," says Henry, reaching into his pocket. "Here's a wire that came from the Chicago office insisting that we finish our reports before tomorrow."

"Let me see that wire." She meets the telegram more than half-way as he hands it over.

"What day is this?" she snaps.

"What day? Why—er—a—Friday—the tenth."

"Well, this wire is dated Thursday the ninth. How do you explain that?" she queries.

Henry looks at the wire. "Well, dear, you see it was a night letter. It was sent from Chicago last night but we didn't receive it until this morning."

"Who else was working with you?" She's boring in.

"Jack!" is Henry's prompt reply.

"Okay. Jack and Lucy are coming over for bridge tomorrow night. I'll see what he has to say. Don't you want something to eat before you go to bed?"

Now *she's* merely open-minded. She'll listen, but she needs a *lot* of evidence.

Suppose, however, the conversation runs something like this:

Henry's here again. His wife calls downstairs.

"Is that you, Henry?"

"Yes, dear," he replies wearily.

"Where have *you* been?. . . Don't you lie to me!" she snarls. (She's at his side now, roping her negligee. Her hair's in curlers. Her lips, too. She leers through eyes nearly closed.)

"Working late at the office, dear," meekly replies this innocent martyr, weak from toil.

But does she listen? No!

"Why . . . you . . . dog! You . . . rat!" Bursting into tears, she waves her fists menacingly, "I'll find out where you *really* were tonight if it's the last thing I do!"

Henry protects his retreat as best he can.

Now there's a *closed mind*. She's thinking negatively in relation to Henry.

You see how easy it is to find out exactly where you stand with anyone. You don't have to be a great psychologist to discern what your position is. All you have to do is to listen to what the other person says.

When a student takes his examination paper to his teacher and implies that he deserves a better grade on the test, and the teacher says, "I'll be glad to review your paper again," the student will know that the teacher's mind is open toward him. So he can check Mental Level No. 2.

But if the teacher says, "You got exactly what you deserve," the student had better check Mental Level No. 1—Closed Mind.

When an employee asks his boss for a raise, and the boss says, "I've had that in mind for some time, Tom. I'll arrange a 10 per cent increase beginning next week," Tom can put his boss on Mental Level No. 4—Belief. But if the boss says, "You ought to be thankful you've got a job," check Mental Level No. 1—Closed Mind.

When a mother counsels her daughter against going on the hayride and her daughter says, "I see what you mean. Okay, Mom," check Mental Level No. 4.

When a disgruntled employee tells his foreman, "Yea . . . you fire me for that and I'll tell the union and there'll be a strike around here," the foreman had better check Mental Level No. 1, for here's an employee whose mind is definitely closed.

When the housewife slams the door in the salesman's face, check Mental Level No. 1.

When a sailor on leave whispers into his sweetheart's ear as they sit in a moon-drenched rowboat in Central Park, and she says, "Yes," check No. 4. If she says, "Maybe," check No. 3. If she says, "I hardly know you," check No. 2. If she slaps his face and says, "Nuts," check No. 1 and tell the sailor to "weigh anchor."

With a closed-minded person, you must first open his mind. A person who is merely open-minded needs plenty of evidence. One who has confidence in you needs only a little evidence. One who believes in you doesn't need any proof at all and as we shall see, it is a grave mistake to go into long explanations with such a person.

In fact, before you can behave intelligently or effectively in your relations with anyone, you must determine exactly where you stand with that person.

If you want to get a measure of where you stand right now in your relations with other people, make a list of some of the people you know—people you live with, work with, call on, or associate with.

How many believe in you?

How many have confidence in you?

How many are open-minded in relation to you?

How many of these minds are closed to you?

Wouldn't you like every one of these people to believe in you? Of course you would. That's what we all want— desperately. When others believe in us, believe what we say, we get what we want and life's a lot more enjoyable.

In the chapters immediately following, you will learn how to open closed minds, gain their confidence, and finally win their belief, which is, by all accounts, the greatest prize in human relations that life has to offer anyone.

CHAPTER III

Opening A Closed Mind

When I graduated from an engineering school and entered the field of educational research, I was under the impression that all I had to do to open the mind of anyone who might oppose me was to (1) be sure I was *right,* and (2) keep pounding my opponent with facts until he saw the light and came around to my point of view.

But I couldn't help noticing that this method wasn't successful.

Even in my social relations—if an untamed Irishman can be said to have any social relations—I found that I was developing a remarkable genius for making people furious.

At this dark hour, it was Professor George H. Follows, master in human relations and Head of the Commercial Engineering Department at Carnegie Institute of Technology, who came to my rescue. It was he who first pointed out to me the universal truth that no matter how right you are, no matter how loaded you are with facts to prove it, agreement with anyone helps to open his mind and opposition tends to close it.

The simplest possible explanation of this is that one of the deepest desires of the human heart is to prove we are right. And anyone who helps you to be right opens not only your mind but your heart.

Everyone wants to be "right." We can't even sleep well

at night until we've satisfied ourselves that we are right, no matter what we did that day.

Until we do so, our subconscious mind keeps banging away at us and we can't get any rest. It's what psychologists have been calling "rationalization" for years.

Even a fellow who commits murder can't eat or sleep until he satisfies himself that he was justified.

So isn't it clear that when you help someone to be right you are satisfying his greatest desire—his greatest need?

No wonder he opens his mind to you!

Think of the people you know. Isn't it true that you open your mind and you do most for those who agree with you and help you to be right? And isn't it equally true that you close your mind to those who oppose you and help you to be wrong?

This simple truth seemed so obvious to me that I began to dream of the possibility of ending all human conflict. For if everyone could be told the secret of opening the other fellow's mind, men could finally reason together on the basis of well-rounded information and arrive at common agreements for the benefit of all concerned.

But then I bumped into one of the doggondest quirks in human nature.

It seems that all of us are subconsciously inclined to help the other fellow to be *wrong* because every time someone else makes a mistake, it makes us feel smart.

We may not be fully aware of it, but we are continually comparing ourselves with others. In these comparisons, we tend to build ourselves up and tear other people down— belittling their appearance, their possessions, or their achievements in order to explain away our own failures or insufficiencies.

Just listen to some of the things that people say every

day in the week, and check up on your own thoughts, and you'll see what I mean.

How often do you hear things like this?

"At least I'm not as fat as she is."

"With all the crazy drivers on the road, it's a wonder we don't have more accidents. Look at that dumb cluck!"

"Sure he makes better marks than I do! But he's a bookworm. He does nothing but study. Nobody likes him."

"Every one of her kids is spoiled. No manners. No discipline. No nothing. What a shock they're going to get when they get out into the world!"

"Let him have his money. Some people get all the breaks."

"He got that job through pull. But I can't understand what holds him up. He's so stupid."

"No wonder he got a raise. He's always licking the boss's boots."

"Well, she finally got him. She ran after him day and night."

So many people never seem to outgrow this childish mental attitude toward others. They continue to gloat over the mistakes, minimize the accomplishments, and use the failures and misfortunes of others as the foundation for their own self-esteem.

Helping others to be wrong—what a cheap and childish method for gaining a feeling of superiority; what a futile way to build up one's ego.

Every sane person can see that his own self-esteem must rest on what he is—not on what someone else isn't.

But before we can stop helping others to be wrong and start helping others to be right, we must overcome our jungle heritage and acquire a more civilized attitude toward people. We must begin to hope that others will *not* make mistakes, will *not* make fools of themselves. We must hope that others will be right and will succeed. And that can be done. But it's not so easy as it looks. It takes practice.

In our attempt to open a person's mind by helping him to be right, mere perfunctory agreement with him is not enough.

For example, on a Riverside Park bench overlooking the Hudson, a young lady who wanted to get married sat with a recalcitrant suitor.

"Do you think my eyes are like the stars?" she asked him.

And he replied, "Yeah."

"And you think my teeth are like a string of pearls?" she continued.

And he said, "Yeah."

"And you think my complexion is like rose petals?"

"Yeah."

"And you think my hair is like spun gold in the moonlight?"

"Yeah."

"Oh, Joe!" she exclaimed. "You say the most wonderful things!"

There's no question about it. "Yes" *is* one of the most wonderful things you can say to anybody. But more intelligent people are likely to get fed up on the sweet perfunctory agreements of "Yes" men. These people want more than agreement before they open their minds to you. They know that it is impossible for you sincerely to agree or disagree with them until you fully understand their point of view. They want you to understand them first and then they want you to agree with them.

Most people feel that they are misunderstood. And they are. They are for the simple reason that rarely does anyone take the time to try to understand them.

Your ability to open a person's mind, then, depends entirely on your mental attitude toward that person—your willingness to understand him and to help him to be right. And opening his mind is your first step toward getting him to believe what you say and do what you want. (See Exhibit I.)

HOW OTHER PEOPLE FEEL ABOUT YOU

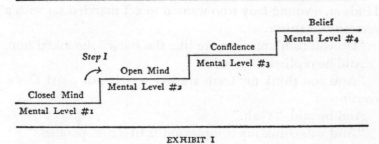

EXHIBIT I

"Yes, Reilly . . . but wait a minute," you say. "You're not going to ask me to help the other fellow to be right when I know he's wrong and I'm right! Suppose parents merely helped their children to do all the crazy things they want to do. What kind of a madhouse would you have for a home? Suppose a corporation executive, negotiating union contracts, always gave the union everything they asked for. How long do you think the corporation would stay in business? Suppose the salesman went around helping all his prospects who don't want to buy to be right. How much business do you think he'd get? Suppose I ask the boss for a raise and he says I don't deserve it. Where do I get off trying to help him to be right? And when some other nation tries to pull a fast one on us, how in the world can we help them to be right?"

Well, you're absolutely right when you say that this attitude of helping others to be right won't get you anywhere— if you stop there.

That's merely the *first step*.

Bear in mind that in this chapter we're dealing with the fellow whose mind is closed and your first job is to try to open his mind *by persuasion*. The conditions under which the use of force might be considered—when persuasion fails —are discussed later on in the book.

The main thing you accomplish when you start out by helping the other person to be right is that you open your *own* mind and make an active effort to put yourself in the other person's place and to really understand why he thinks the way he does.

When you do this, and are perfectly sincere about it, the other person is much more likely to open his mind and to listen to *your* side of the question.

In the process, you may learn something that changes your thinking, and the other fellow may too.

When you open you own mind and approach a question from the other fellow's point of view, you have a good chance to round out a complete picture of the facts and to find out and admit it if the other fellow's right and you're wrong in some respects. And once you prove yourself capable of doing this, the other fellow is inclined to want to prove that he's capable of being just as fair and just as open-minded as you are—with the result that he will see and admit points where you are right and he's wrong.

As you know, whenever any two people open their minds —each to the other's side—they are well on the way toward a common agreement. On the other hand, two closed-minded people may argue forever and not arrive anywhere.

Getting down to cases, you can classify your everyday situations as they come up, under one of three main headings:

1. Sometimes you're right and the other fellow's wrong.
2. Sometimes you're partly right and the other fellow's partly right.

3. Sometimes you're wrong and the other fellow's right.

Now offhand, you'd say that it just doesn't make sense to help the other fellow to be right when you know he's really wrong. And again, offhand, you'd say that you should be most willing to help the other fellow to be right when he really is right, and you know you're wrong.

Well, let's see.

WHAT TO DO WHEN YOU'RE RIGHT AND THE OTHER FELLOW'S WRONG

Grownups think much the same as children. The main difference is that grownups have learned to cover up their thoughts more and say what they don't think.

So let's lead off with a child's case that clearly reveals what to do and what not to do when you're right and the other person's wrong.

Some months ago, at our house, we had vegetable soup for dinner—homemade vegetable soup.

My wife made it and every member of the family had something nice to say about it . . . "Delicious!" . . . "Best I've ever tasted!" . . . "What flavor!" . . . everyone, that is, but our seven-year-old boy.

He just sat there—wouldn't touch it.

"What's the matter with you?" I inquired.

"I don't like vegetable soup," he replied, without even looking up.

Now I believed that I was right in feeling that this boy, like the rest of our children, should learn to eat what's put in front of him—especially healthful foods such as vegetable soup. So I proceeded to tell him so.

"How can you say you don't like *this* vegetable soup when you haven't even tasted it?" I argued.

"I don't like *any* vegetable soup," was his pat reply.

"Why . . . everybody likes vegetable soup," I countered

excitedly. "It's one of the most healthful and delicious dishes you can eat. It has everything in it. It's full of vitamins. Makes you grow. Makes you strong."

"Well, *I* don't like vegetable soup," was his firm position.

"Well, you're going to eat it," I commanded. "If you don't understand how to eat with the rest of the family, take that dish of vegetable soup into the playroom and don't come back until it's finished."

So the boy marched off to the playroom with his vegetable soup.

Soon we had all finished our soup and the main course was served. But there was no report from the boy in the playroom. I got up from the table, walked down the hall into the playroom, and there he sat.

The soup hadn't been touched.

His mind (and his mouth) were closed to vegetable soup.

Before I had a chance to open my mouth, he said, "You know, Dad, you can't *force* someone to like vegetable soup. That's not straight thinking." (He had picked up that last sentence from me.)

That was enough for me.

Even though I still felt that I was right and he was wrong, it was apparent that up to this point I was getting nowhere for the simple reason that I was helping him to be wrong. That merely closed his mind. When this dawned on me, I immediately decided to reopen his mind by helping him to be right.

"You're right, boy," I admitted. "I just made a mistake. Pass it up this time. Come on and eat the rest of your dinner. We'll talk about vegetable soup some other time. Okay?"

"Okay, Dad."

Later, when I took him up to bed, *he* reopened the subject.

When I kissed him good night, he put his little hand over on my arm, and said, reassuringly, "Dad . . . you don't have to worry about making that mistake at dinner."

That opened up quite a man-to-man talk, and he seemed fairly receptive to my reasonably complete review of all the healthful advantages of eating vegetable soup.

"I just went about it the wrong way," I concluded. "But there must be some answer. There must be *some* way to get you to like vegetable soup. And I want you to help me to find that way."

Suddenly the boy offered a solution. "Do you know how to get me to like it?" he said eagerly.

"How?" said I, with bated breath.

"Just don't have it for a long, long time," he counseled. "Then I'll get to like it. That's how I got to like spinach."

Then I remembered that I had felt the same way at one time about tapioca pudding.

"Another thing, Dad," he continued, "you see, you're lucky! You're married!"

"And what's that got to do with it?" I inquired.

"Why—you *never* have to eat what *you* don't like! All you have to do is tell Mommy what you want for dinner, and you get it. What do I have to do—wait till I get married before I can get what I like?"

"No, boy. You don't have to wait till you get married," I told him. "What do you want for dinner tomorrow night?"

Now he *was* interested. Now his mind *was* open—wide open.

Cube steak (that's the inexpensive Irish cut), string beans, mashed potatoes and ice cream with chocolate sauce and nuts, was his selection.

"Okay . . . that's what we'll have. Come to think of it, each one in the family can have a turn saying what he wants, and that will solve one of the greatest problems that Mommy has, because she's always wondering what she'll have for dinner. But if we eat what you like tomorrow night, will you eat what Mommy likes on Tuesday night, and what Ann likes on Wednesday night, and what Myrtle likes on Thursday night, and what I like on Friday night?"

The boy agreed wholeheartedly.

So it's apparent to me, and I know by this time it must be to you, that it takes plenty of practice before we develop the necessary patience to help the other fellow to be right— especially when we're convinced at the outset that we are right and he's wrong.

But by helping this child to be right (even though I felt he was wrong) I opened his mind.

And not only that.

Once his mind was opened, he willingly helped me to be right and offered a solution that cleared up the whole problem.

Today he eats vegetable soup when it's served—and likes it.

True, I could have used force to *make* him eat it. But he wouldn't have *liked* it. And more important, he wouldn't have liked *me*.

In most of our everyday relations with grownups, we can't *force* them to do what we want them to do—even if we're right and they're wrong.

We must *persuade* them.

Even in those exceptional instances when force is necessary, and when conditions are such that force can *safely* be used, it should be used only as a last resort, after persuasion has failed. Therefore, before we can intelligently and effectively and safely use the implements of force, discussed in Chapter VII, we must first master the principles of persuasion. And you haven't a ghost of a chance to persuade a closed mind. You must first open it.

The director of an amateur theatrical told me of an instance in which he saved his star act by helping two young ladies to be right when he knew very well they were wrong.

These two ingenues had achieved quite a reputation for themselves, locally, for singing in harmony while one played the piano. In this amateur show, they were to have their big moment in a cabaret scene, accompanied by a professional orchestra.

At rehearsal they both stopped in the middle of their number and complained that they were so accustomed to working with their own piano accompaniment, they did not feel they could do themselves justice with the orchestra accompanying them.

The director said that he was afraid that this would hold up the show and ruin the entire effect if a couple of inexperienced stagehands interrupted the act to roll a piano into position on the stage.

"They insisted, however," the director told me, "that they could not do their number unless they had their own piano. Even though I knew they were wrong, I arranged to follow their wishes, asking four male members of the cast to act as stagehands, leaving their assigned places on the stage and going behind the wings to roll out the piano and roll it off again at the end of their number.

"The dress rehearsal was run off. Everyone saw that the show was stopped cold when this piano shifting took place. However, I made no complaint or comment. After the dress rehearsal, both young ladies came to me and explained that they believed I was correct, and for the sake of the show they would be willing to sing to the accompaniment of the orchestra. As it turned out, their number was the hit of the show."

One of the most successful advertising space salesmen I know told me that he had called on a prospect for years and was absolutely convinced that the prospect should buy.

But he never did.

The prospect contended that he was perfectly satisfied with the magazines he was using, that he had tested them out through the years, and that he saw no sense in taking a chance on any new ones.

The salesman had worn himself out trying to prove, with facts and figures, that he was right and the prospect was wrong.

One day the salesman got so weary that he changed his tactics.

"I'm convinced," he told the prospect, "that you ought to be using my magazine. But apparently you're right and I'm wrong. You see, I'm on a tough spot. My boss expects me to sell you. I'd almost be willing to pay for a test ad myself, just to see whether it pays out. Maybe I've been wrong in trying to sell you my magazine at all if those other magazines you're using pay out so much better."

As soon as the salesman stopped trying to prove the prospect was wrong, the pressure was off.

"Well," said the prospect, "I guess neither one of us can really be sure until we test it out. Okay, we'll try a small test ad."

The test ad paid out and the prospect turned into a regular customer.

However, even when a salesman succeeds in getting a prospect to test his product, he's not always over the hump. For when test results seem unfavorable, the prospect's mind closes up again—tighter than ever. And the salesman has got to re-open it all over again.

A salesman of industrial oils and greases persuaded a large textile manufacturer to try out a high-quality grease in their spinning plant.

When he called to find out how they liked it, the purchasing agent advised that the grease was too hard to feed through their grease guns.

The salesman immediately produced facts and figures, supported by scientific laboratory tests, which proved that the purchasing agent must be wrong. But the argument only wound up with the purchasing agent's final "Sorry, but your grease just didn't test out for us."

The whole thing bothered the salesman so much that he didn't sleep very well that night. Next morning he decided on a new approach.

"I'm sorry, too, that our test was a flop," he told the purchasing agent. "But maybe we can learn something. I'd like to examine the grease guns and find out why our grease failed"

The purchasing agent's mind was wide open now. He introduced the salesman to the overseer on the night shift who had complained about the grease being too hard. And a full investigation revealed that the worker who brought the grease from the supply room had gotten the wrong grease.

Yes, there's a right time and a wrong time to use facts and figures. There's no use trying to use proof material on a mind that's closed. You've got to open it first. And the best way to open anyone's mind is to help him to be right.

A struggling young junior executive in a large national organization told me, "Every time I do a brilliant job, the boss tries to hog all the credit. He's one of these selfish birds who's always building himself up with the general manager. I'm fed up. First chance I get I'm going to quit and tell him what I think of him."

'The same problem you recite," I told him, "is found in practically every organization in the world, and I'm sure you must realize that you can't solve this problem by running away from it and securing a position elsewhere.

"Let's assume that you're right and the boss is wrong and selfish. Nevertheless, no matter what a man's position is in business, his most important job in human relations is to get the active support and sponsorship of his immediate superior. And the one sure way to win this sponsorship is to help that immediate superior to accomplish *his* objectives.

"Let's grant that some of these objectives are selfish. Let's recognize at the outset that your boss is very much interested in protecting his position against you or any other member of your department, and the smarter you are, the more necessary it becomes for him to protect his position against you.

"If you were the head of your department, reporting to the general manager of the business, then the general manager, whether he realized it or not, would be interested in protecting his position against you. If you were the general manager, then the president would be interested in protecting his position against your competition.

"And that's the way it goes. No matter how far up the ladder we go, we can never hope to escape this realistic human problem. However, it is primary in all human relations that if you help someone to be right and assist him to achieve his objectives, you are much more likely to get his support and his sponsorship than if you openly compete with him and threaten the achievement of his objectives.

"Ordinarily it is very rare for a man in any organization to secure a promotion by leaping over the head of his immediate superior. A man's promotion usually consists of filling the shoes of his immediate superior, when he in turn moves up to fill his boss's place. And it is difficult for one to receive such a promotion without the active sponsorship of his immediate superior.

"Even if you try to escape this problem by moving to another company, you can't very well do it without the recommendation of your present boss.

"This isn't a matter of playing petty company politics. 'Helping the other fellow to be right' and to achieve his objectives, no matter how selfish he may be, is simply sound human relations, because it demonstrates an unselfish desire to serve the other fellow, and I have never met anyone who did not respond favorably to this kind of treatment."

Within six months this young man reported to me that he had secured a raise.

And an executive, a little farther up the line, who was experiencing the same kind of "boss trouble," and who adopted this same helping-the-boss-to-be-right attitude for correcting it, wrote me, saying, "The situation has been eased a lot. 'Helping the other fellow to be right' is heap good medicine!"

These cases are typical of hundreds of instances I've observed first-hand in counseling young men with their career problems.

The managing director of a trade association told me, "We get all kinds of unreasonable requests from members. If we granted all of them, we'd go broke. Nevertheless, whenever I get a letter asking us to do several things, I invariably try to find something in that letter that we *can* do.

"Then I begin my reply with the sentence, 'Yes, Mr. Blank, you are right.' Whenever I am able to start a letter that way, I know I will open the other fellow's mind to the reasons why we can't do everything he asks."

Suppose you order ham and eggs and the waitress brings you turtle soup. If you say, "Pardon me, I guess I didn't make myself clear," the waitress will readily admit that she's wrong, think you're a very swell guy, and get your ham and eggs in a hurry.

If, on the other hand, you say what you would be perfectly justified in saying, "Hey . . . what's the big idea? Can't you understand English?" the waitress will then think, "Nuts to you," and you may find yourself waiting a long time for your ham and eggs.

Any good salesman will tell you that even if he's 100 per cent right and the prospect is 100 per cent wrong, this isn't enough to assure him of an order. "Winning an argument and losing a sale" is so common that any salesman worthy of the name will readily agree that "thinking with the prospect" and "helping him to be right" is the first step toward more sales and more profits.

As Charles M. Schwab, master of human relations, said, "Many of us think of salesmen as people traveling around with sample kits. Instead, we are all salesmen every day of our lives. We are selling our ideas, our plans, our energies, our enthusiasm to those with whom we come in contact."[1]

So it appears that even when we know we're right, and the other fellow's absolutely wrong, our best chance to get what we want is to open the other fellow's mind by helping him to be right.

However, let's be honest with ourselves.

Sometimes we're only partly right and partly wrong.

What to do then?

WHAT TO DO WHEN YOU'RE PARTLY RIGHT

Your best chance to get anyone to admit he's made a mistake, is to begin by admitting that maybe you made one yourself.

Years ago, Benjamin Franklin offered the following counsel:

The way to convince another is to state your case moderately and accurately. Then scratch your head, or shake it a little and say that is the way it seems to you, but that of course you may be mistaken about it; which causes your listener to receive what you have to say, and as like as not, turn about and try to convince you of it, since you are in doubt. But if you go at him in a tone of positiveness and arrogance you only make an opponent of him.

[1] *Strategy in Handling People,* by Ewing Webb and John Morgan (New York: Garden City Pub. Co., Inc.), 1932.

I know an able young sales promotion manager who had battled with his boss for a raise for years and got nowhere for the simple reason that he felt that he was getting a raw deal and was always trying to prove that his boss was a tightwad.

He was right in desiring a raise, but his boss was also right in feeling that he was getting paid all he was worth.

I saw this same young man secure a substantial raise after he had reversed his mental attitude toward the boss.

The moment he began "helping the boss to be right" he found himself actively trying to figure out why the boss thought that way. In effect, he told his employer, "When you say I don't deserve a raise, that is of vital interest to me, for I know you usually have very sound reasons for anything you say. So I'd appreciate your letting me know from time to time how I can go about making myself more valuable to you so that in your judgment I'll really deserve a raise."

By this simple reversal of his mental attitude, the young promotion manager not only enlisted his boss's support and help in making himself more valuable, but he opened his employer's mind to all the evidence he had to present indicating why his pay should be increased.

When we open our minds to the other fellow's point of view, our education really begins.

Yes, whenever I get a "raw deal" from anyone, all I have to do in order to get at the real reason is to take a good look at myself in the mirror.

A husband, observing his wife's new hat and coat, went into a pout. When she asked him what the trouble was, he exploded.

He accused her of being extravagant and careless with his money. "We used to get along nicely on $300 a month," he barked. "Now we hardly seem able to get by on $400."

After the smoke of battle had cleared away, and both of them had said a lot of nasty things they didn't mean, which left his wife in a sobbing spell, he found himself defeated and considerably embarrassed. He had temporarily over-looked certain obvious facts—that two new children had been born in the family since "they used to get along on $300," that they were living in a more expensive home now, that he was smoking more expensive cigars now, that he was spending more for his lunches than he used to, that *he* was buying better clothes, that they had a better car, that they were entertaining more, and so on all the way along the line.

If, instead of starting out with the idea that his wife was entirely at fault, he had begun by admitting some of his own "extravagances," she would have more willingly admitted hers. The time wasted in a nasty quarrel could have been used more productively, reviewing the facts and discussing the best ways and means of cutting expenses. Then there wouldn't have been any problem left—except trying to get along on $400 a month.

"Five minutes *after* I left the board room," explained the advertising manager of a large organization, "I thought of what I *should* have said. You see, I had carefully prepared my whole plan, and I knew it was right. But I was so eager to get my program approved, that I immediately opposed the sales manager who suggested a change. *Now* I can see that he was right, too. And what's more, I could have accepted his suggested change without damaging my program one bit. In fact, the suggested change would have helped it.

"If I had only told him that in the meeting, he would have gone along with me on the rest of the program.

"I just need more practice in helping the other fellow to be right in tough situations."

A young married man with two children nearly lost his job because, in a fit of temper, he had called the boss "unfair." "I know . . . I shouldn't have said what I did," he told me. "But when the boss tried to pin all the blame on me, I got sore and tried to deny that I was at fault at all. What I should have done was to admit I was partly to blame. Then there wouldn't have been any argument at all. My trouble is I can't hide my true feelings."

"When you have a pain in your stomach, your most important job is not to *hide* that pain, but to *get rid of it.* Isn't that right?" I asked.

And he agreed.

"Well, the same idea is true when you are troubled with an antagonistic feeling toward someone else," I told him. "Don't try to hide it. Try to get rid of it. And the one sure way to get rid of your mental pains and to 'feel right' about your boss or anyone else is to get into the mental habit of helping him to be right."

I talk to so many fellows who never seem to get anywhere because they are so much smarter than the people who run things. George Jessel, popular comedian, expressed the point pretty well when he told Moss Hart about the inefficiency of a certain movie magnate. "I told him how to run his studio," concluded Jessel.

"Then what happened?" asked Hart.

"Oh, nothing," said George. "We parted good friends. He boarded his yacht and I took the subway home."

As I commented to one young man who had just finished telling me how stupid his boss was, "Your boss must have something on the ball. After all, he *is* your boss. He makes more money than you do. If you only helped him to be right, you'd probably find some things to admire in him. If you admire him, you'll show it. Takes a little practice . . . that's all. Try it . . . for your own advancement."

In our social relations, we often forget ourselves and yield to the momentary temptation to deflate someone who "burns us up" with a superior attitude. After such an occasion, I overheard one husband say to his wife, "You didn't have to say *that* to her!"

"Well, what do I care for her?" answered the wife. "She's not important."

"I know she's not important," countered the husband. "but what you said was indelicate—that's all . . . in fact, it sounded like hell!"

This same woman, earlier in the evening, was whipping an absentee over the bridge table. "Why—she can't get away with that! Who does she think she is? I just *hate* to hurt her feelings, but believe me, the next time I see her, I'm going to tell her a thing or two."

This woman and her twin sister in every social set remind me of the farmer who said he went to town every Saturday night to get drunk, and oh, how he dreaded it!

This woman enjoys her emotional sprees—helping other people to be wrong, just as much as the farmer enjoyed getting drunk on Saturday night. The main difference is that the farmer's suffering is over with by Monday, while this woman suffers from a perpetual mental hangover. She is destined to become a social outcast for the simple reason that she is addicted to the vicious daily habit of giving her ego a cheap but temporary "jag" by blindly helping the other person to be wrong and satisfying herself that she's right.

The next time you find yourself feeling pretty mad after a day at the office or a day with the children or an afternoon at bridge or an evening with the Joneses, stop and review exactly what happened. You'll probably find that you are simply suffering from the mental hangover that invariably follows the emotional spree of helping someone to be wrong.

There's a sign in a Lincoln, Nebraska café that reads, "Tomato juice, aspirin, black coffee, and our sympathy . . 15c."

Be assured of my sympathy. Take tomato juice, aspirin,

and black coffee if you wish. But the one sure way to shake it off is to change your mental attitude toward that person and help him to be right.

Day after day in the course of my business contacts, I hear little men with controversial attitudes disagreeing with other people—helping them to be wrong, and I hear big men with open minds flowing with other people, helping them to be right.

Sitting in the office of a minor assistant, I heard him bawl out an office boy who had delivered a package to the wrong place. Apparently it never occurred to this assistant that his instructions might not have been clear.

Sitting in the office of this minor assistant's boss, I heard this major executive excuse a branch manager for having made a blunder. "Perhaps my memorandum wasn't as clear as it should have been," he told him.

We all know it is little people who give us the most trouble. The fundamental reason why they give us so much trouble is that they're always trying to appear 100 per cent right, and doing everything they can to help us be 100 per cent wrong. These little people have a very poor chance of enjoying life.

You can pretty well predict any man's or any woman's success or failure on the basis of what he or she says to others in the course of everyday conversations.

Those who fail can tell you what's wrong with everyone.

Those who succeed can tell you what's right about them.

Check up and you'll find that the most popular and the most successful member of any business or social set, male or female, is the one who's willing to admit his own faults, and look for the good points in others.

One of the most successful business executives I know tells everyone who works for him, "I don't want to hear any criticisms about anyone who works here. Any time you can pass on a compliment about someone I'm always glad to hear it."

This trains his employees to look for the good points in their associates, instead of their faults. When they do this, naturally everyone gets along better, and spends more time in productive work, less time in destructive argument and gossip

Another chief executive who has done an amazing job of transforming a run-down company into an outstanding success, instructs his department heads to submit every Monday morning a report of all the *good* things that have happened in his department during the preceding week.

WHAT TO DO WHEN YOU'RE ENTIRELY WRONG— AND YOU KNOW IT

Every now and then, a situation arises when you are entirely wrong—and you know it.

What to do then?

Believe it or not, the more wrong we are, the more difficult it is for us to admit it.

You'd think that when we're 100 per cent wrong and the other fellow is 100 per cent right, we should be willing to help him to be right.

But we're not.

When I was nineteen years old, I had a job in a Youngstown steel mill—assistant timekeeper. My job was to go around the mill every morning and every afternoon and check off every employee. But I had to *see* a workman before I checked his name. For the first few weeks I had lots of fun climbing around furnaces, looking through tunnels, and searching the far corners of the mill until I had *actually seen* every last man. But after a while I began to get a little careless. Sometimes men were working up behind a huge furnace and I couldn't see them all. Instead of going up, I developed the habit of calling to some workman I could see and asking him who else was up there. Late one afternoon the boss called me in.

"I see you have Martin checked in for today," he said, holding up a copy of my morning report.

"Yes, sir. He was here this morning," was my quick comeback.

"He was like hell. You took another man's word for it. You didn't *see* him. He wasn't here."

"What do you expect me to do," I countered, "risk my life climbing around a furnace to see a man?"

"Oh, so that's the way you look at it, huh? You're going to stand there and defend yourself when you made a mistake. You're going to tell me that it's all right to check a man present when he's absent. You don't know the first principles about your job. If you're afraid to climb around furnaces, we can get a man who will. You're fired."

That evening I didn't feel like eating much supper. That night I did a lot of thinking. Was I sore? For the first few hours I couldn't think of an appropriate name to fit that big gorilla of a boss. How would *he* like to climb around furnaces and crawl through stinking tunnels—why, the big ham! Who wants to work for a bully like him anyhow?

But there were two things he said to me that I couldn't get out of my mind: "You're going to stand there and defend yourself when you made a mistake," and "You don't know the first principles about your job." These two sentences kept banging away at me until I finally had to admit to myself that I was wrong about the whole thing. I got to sleep about 3 A.M.

The next morning I went to see the boss. "You certainly did the right thing when you fired me," I began. "I was dead wrong. But what's worse—I was too pigheaded to see it and admit it. I learned more about my job last night in two hours than I learned working on the job for two months. Last night for the first time, I realized what a time-keeper is supposed to do. I want to thank you for waking me up. I'm going to look for a new job today, and thanks to you, I'll never make the mistake again of defending myself when I'm wrong. If I'm ever fired again—that won't be the reason."

And to my surprise, the boss said, "If you mean that, take off your coat and go to work."

Now it would have been easy for me, in the early stages of this affair, right after I was fired, to develop a grudge for that boss and to carry it for the rest of my life. My first thoughts were right along that line. For that's when we are most likely to develop our grudges—when we're dead wrong.

It's easier to develop a grudge against someone than it is to admit you've been a sap. And, after all, a pet hate is a great diversion.

When you come right down to it, it's true that many people—many of the people you know—would be barren of any personality whatsoever if you took all their pet peeves and grand grudges away from them. They're at their "best" when they're riding their favorite hate.

Even when you've been handed a raw deal—even when you're right and the other fellow's wrong—the best thing to do is to get mad and to get over it.

But when you're right and the other fellow's wrong, you don't get so mad as you do when you're wrong and the other fellow's right. For when you're wrong, you're fearful. And fear is the mother of bitterness. When you admit you're wrong and try to make amends, your fears vanish. But when you stubbornly refuse to admit your mistake, your sub-conscious fears keep growing and giving birth to bitterness which soon becomes an obsession.

Whenever you fall victim to bitterness or hate, and allow yourself to harbor a grudge, it's just too bad for *you*, because it hurts you far more than it does the other fellow.

In the first place, your pet hate provides a perfect emotional escape from the facts of life. It paralyzes and freezes your mind so that you are unable to reason, blinds you so that you cannot see the mistakes you have made, and relieves you of any realization on your part of the steps you should take to improve yourself.

Second, your pet hate runs you down physically. It makes you nervous, gives you a sour stomach, and the first thing you know your face has taken on a sour expression.

Third, the germ of hate has tremendous powers of reproduction, and the person who encourages it will soon find himself in possession of a full-blown "persecution" complex. You know people like that—people who feel that they can't trust anybody and that the world has handed them all the bum breaks and dirty deals. In extreme cases, it leads to insanity. And pathological haters are to be avoided like a plague.

No one who holds grudges can call himself mentally healthy. Certainly it's impossible for you to open anyone's mind if you harbor hate or bitterness for that person.

You can't even afford to walk into any human relation with a chip on your shoulder.

I know the manager of a well-known orchestra who was "called on the carpet" before a labor leader.

He ironed out the whole difficulty in a one-hour meeting with the union chief, largely because he started the interview by saying, "I want to explain certain mistakes we've been making in our dealings with the union, and how we came to make them."

"I was wrong."

"I made a mistake."

Tough words to say. But they do open the other fellow's mind.

We all masquerade too much.

We are all inclined to put on the false whiskers and try to act like Superman. Up until the time I was fired from that job in Youngstown, I always thought that the most important thing in the world was to be right, and that the best way to get the admiration and respect and affection of others was to share your rightness with them and to set them straight.

More than anything else I wanted to be right. I wanted others to think that I was right, so naturally when I made a mistake I thought that the best thing to do was to cover it up as quickly and completely as possible so that others would not find it out.

Apparently it never dawned on me that everyone else wanted to be right, too, and that my desire to be right was only one little part of all the desires of humanity.

I never got the admiration and respect and affection that I thought I'd get by acting like the perfect man, and I never fully understood why until I accidentally stumbled on it with that boss in Youngstown. Up to that time, I satisfied myself that other people refused to listen to my rightness because they were just a bunch of dummies who had no sincere desire to learn. But when that boss in Youngstown finally caught me red-handed,—failing to do the thing that I was hired to do—there was a mistake that I couldn't possibly cover up or laugh off, and it was entirely for the good of my own soul and peace of mind that I decided to go back, after I was fired, and tell him so.

That was when I accidentally discovered the great truth that it is possible for a person actually to build character for himself and to enjoy the cooperation of others in a measure never before realized, merely by admitting that he has made a mistake. And I have used that fundamental truth many times since.

After all, no one can ever succeed in appearing perfect— or be happy trying to.

We all want to be loved and respected for what we really are—well-meaning but *im*perfect.

We would all like to quit the false and futile attitude of trying to appear infallible. We're willing to admit that we make mistakes—if others would only do the same.

Trouble is, we all expect the other fellow to admit his mistakes *first*.

If you will only take the initiative and stop trying to act as if you were always right, others will usually admit their weaknesses.

It's all as simple as that.

So it seems that in practically all our relations with others, whether we're 100 per cent right, partly right, or 100 per cent wrong, the one sure way to open the other fellow's mind is to begin by helping him to be right.

One of the best ways to find out how you like something is to try it yourself. So before you pass final judgment on the idea of helping the other fellow to be right, try it out yourself. See how it feels.

"I'm sold," you say, "on the proposition of helping the other fellow to be right when he really is right. But when he is wrong, and I know it, I can't stand the idea of treating him as if he were right. For if there is anything I hate, it's flattery."

And I agree with you 100 per cent in taking this position.

I don't mean for one minute that you should engage in any form of hypocritical flattery.

Most people are reluctant about using any form of flattery. They inherently resent the idea of giving the other fellow a big build-up that he doesn't deserve.

Certainly undue praise is to be avoided because it really doesn't express your true feelings. Furthermore, it is dangerous because sooner or later it is detected and it acts as a boomerang against you.

Before you can say anything complimentary to anyone— and be sincere about it—you must first get yourself into the proper frame of mind.

When you start out with the sincere desire to see something *right* about the other fellow's point of view, you automatically open your own mind to the good things about him that you can sincerely commend.

Superficial or insincere approval is never enough, for the simple reason that people want you to understand them fully and have good, solid reasons for commending them. This is impossible if you fail to take the necessary time to explore their side of the question.

No matter how right you think you are, there is a pretty good chance that the other fellow is not a total moron, and he may have something to say to support himself which would influence your final judgment.

It may well be, however, that as you mentally try on the idea of helping the other fellow to be right in your own personal assortment of problem cases, you will dig up at least one situation—perhaps more—that seems hopeless, as far as any kind of persuasion is concerned. And I agree that every now and then we do encounter persons or groups who do not seem to respond to persuasion, even though we extend ourselves in every way possible to help them to be right.

But as we have already pointed out, the use of force is always dangerous and should not be considered until you have first exhausted all hope of persuasion. A thorough understanding of the psychology of persuasion is a necessary prerequisite to the safe and intelligent use of force. Furthermore, there are certain specific conditions which must be present before the use of force can be considered to achieve our objectives with any degree of safety.

So let's postpone, until Chapter VII, our consideration of force. Meanwhile, let's go on with the next step in the psychology of persuasion. Once you've opened a person's mind, by helping him to be right, about all you can be sure of is that you have a "hearing." What you say and do from there on determines whether you gain his confidence or close up his mind again.

CHAPTER IV

Winning Confidence

Once you've opened a person's mind, the best way to win his confidence is by giving him evidence that you *deserve* it. And that's Step 2 in persuading him to believe what you say and do what you want. (See Exhibit II.)

There's nothing mysterious about gaining a person's confidence. It depends on our everyday thoughts and actions in little things as well as big things.

Day in and day out, in casual relations and vital relations with others, we are continually in the process of either gaining or losing the confidence of those who open their minds to us

HOW OTHER PEOPLE FEEL ABOUT YOU

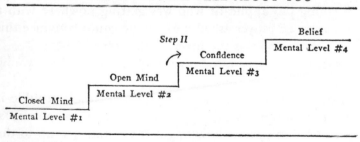

EXHIBIT II

Their estimate of us either rises or falls depending on what we think, what we say, what we do. Hundreds of instances—some of major, some of minor importance—race through my mind; instances that include the small talk of a big executive at leisure trying to make conversation with a client, the serious words of a job applicant trying to impress a prospective employer, the fleeting question of a little boy to a busy father, the overanxiety of a young man trying to get ahead, the sales talk of an insurance representative who had been granted an open-minded interview, the bewildered children of a hurried divorce, the sailor who took me out on a blind date, the mother who broke her promise.

Whenever you feed an open-minded person with favorable evidence, you gain his confidence, for anyone is favorably impressed when you show him that you are thinking and acting in terms of *his* interests as well as your own.

If, after observing the other person's interests—in the process of helping him to be right—you honestly believe that it is to his advantage for him to do what you want him to do, that belief will do more than anything else I know of to gain his confidence.

But in presenting your evidence, be sure to tell him what *he's* going to get out of it, if he does as you suggest.

THINK OF THE OTHER FELLOW'S INTERESTS

A young job applicant who was getting nowhere with a prospective employer asked me how he could convince this employer that *he* was the man for the job.

"Is this employer's mind open to you?" I asked my young friend.

"Yes, I'm sure of it," he replied. "The whole trouble is that the employer's mind is open to several other applicants, too, and I don't know how to get his confidence up to the point where he will select *me*. I want this job and I want it bad."

"Well, just forget about what *you* want for a moment," I told him, "and begin thinking about what the employer wants. Go to this employer and ask him to tell you exactly what kind of a man he's looking for. Then you'll have to be perfectly honest, with him and with yourself, in trying to determine whether or not your qualifications fit in with what he wants. Don't present yourself as 'the perfect answer.' There are no perfect answers. Tell him what your strengths are and tell him what your weaknesses are, in terms of what he's looking for. Tell him that you're not trying to sell him something that you haven't got. Then ask him if any other applicant is better qualified for the job than you are. If so, tell him to hire that man—not you—because that's what you would do if you were in his shoes. But if no other applicant is better fitted for the job than you are, tell him that you want that job, and that you feel it is in his best interests to hire you."

My young friend did just that, and he landed the job.

No matter what you're trying to sell, you don't have to present a "perfect" case in order to make your sale. All you have to do is to show a person that it is to *his* advantage to do what you want him to do—that the advantages of following your suggestion overbalance whatever disadvantages there may be.

In fact, one of the most important steps in gaining anyone's confidence is for you to take him into *your* confidence and help him to anticipate and understand the disadvantages, as well as the advantages, involved in doing what you ask him to do.

It's a mistake for you to wait and let him find out for himself what's wrong with your proposition. Too many people wait until we find things out for ourselves before they "take us into their confidence."

A colored minstrel on the old Keith circuit illustrated the point well when he told this stirring story about his loving mother.

"She was a wonderful mother," he said. "We had fourteen children in our family and no matter what happened, Mother always took us into her confidence. I was only six at the time, but I remember it as if it was yesterday. Mother called all us children around her at the back door. Father was lying across the threshold. 'Children,' she said, simply, 'your father's drunk.'

"Now I think that was perfectly wonderful of Mother to take all us children into her confidence like that. We all thought he was *dead*."

Yes, it's a little late to "take a person into your confidence" and tell him "what's wrong with the horse" after he's bought it and found out for himself. If your proposal is sound, you need not be afraid to tell the other fellow *all* you know about it—including the disadvantages—for by doing so you help gain his confidence. And you can't lose so long as the advantages are important enough to overbalance the disadvantages.

It's easy for you to "put one over" on an open mind . . . *once*. And unless you spend your time thinking in terms of the other fellow's interests, as well as your own, you may find yourself inadvertently taking advantage of him. Whenever this happens, it's just too bad for *you*.

It's easy for a salesman to yield to the temptation of recommending the "buy" that gives him the largest commission, but if that sale turns out to the disadvantage of the buyer, he's lost a good customer.

A salesman, or anyone else, can study the tricks of the trade and acquire a pleasing personality that opens people's minds and persuades them to act, but if the person who acts later regrets his action, the salesman, or anyone else, has an enemy on his hands instead of a friend.

Even though he may not recognize it, a butcher, a baker, a smooth politician, a salesman, a lawyer, and even a physician, may be more interested in what he gets than in what he gives, and when others see evidence of this, they lose confidence.

But if you can overcome this human tendency we all have, of thinking primarily in terms of our own immediate selfish interests; if you can sell yourself on the proposition that in the long run your own self-interests are best served by fully protecting the interests of others as well, your heart is more likely to be in the right place and it is easier for you to say and do the things that gain the lasting confidence of others.

People want to have confidence in you. They don't want to go to the endless trouble of checking and double-checking everything you say.

Life is altogether too complex to permit us to check up on every possible angle before we act. People are hired, goods and services are bought, directions are followed, fortunes change hands, lives are pledged, simply because people have confidence in others.

SELECT THE RIGHT TIME TO PRESENT YOUR EVIDENCE

No matter how fully you consider the other person's interests, no matter how much you *deserve* his confidence, there's a right time and a wrong time to present your evidence.

If you're talking to a hungry man, don't try to convince him of anything until after you've fed him.

If you're talking to someone who's tired, you'd better wait until he's rested.

If you encounter a person who's in a huff about something, you'd better wait until he cools off.

Most people are easier to get along with when they are fresh, relaxed, properly fed, and at leisure than they are when they are tense, tired, hungry, or in a hurry.

There is a right time and a wrong time to ask anyone for

a favor. Everyone has his "moments." And it's up to you to be patient and bide your time until those moments come.

People give you clear and unmistakable signals that tell you when to present your evidence and when not to.

One afternoon in the home of a friend who had been having some difficulty with his teen-age boy, I was all primed to get into conversation with this flaming youth—waiting my chance to open up the subject *my* way. I had no more than opened my mouth to speak, when he beat me to the conversational punch with, "D'ya know any wisecracks?"

I immediately sensed that what I had planned to say to this child would have been improperly timed. So I dusted off a few wisecracks. In fact, we spent all the allotted time with wisecracks—I picking up a few new ones—and we never did get down to business. But I left his mind open. I'll get a good chance at him some day.

"How's business?" I asked the president of a large manufacturing company.

"This year," he replied, "we are enjoying the biggest sales and profits in our history, and for the first six months of this year we'll be lucky if we can fill our presents orders."

That was enough to persuade me that this would be a poor time to present an idea I had for increasing their sales.

This matter of timing is important in all kinds of human situations. It's so easy to say the right thing at the wrong time. And plenty of practice in timing your presentation of evidence pays handsome dividends.

GIVE THE OTHER FELLOW A REASONABLY COMPLETE STATEMENT OF YOUR CASE

One of the best reasons for selecting the right time to present your evidence is that you want to be sure to have sufficient time to present a reasonably complete statement of your case.

A little information is a dangerous thing, and it is a mistake for us to expect to gain the confidence of an open mind unless we fully inform that open mind.

Each of us is engaged day in and day out in selling ideas to others. The man who is attempting to progress 'n his work, the wife who is trying to get the approval of her husband on the purchase of an oil burner or a new coat, the man who is trying to get members for the golf club, the woman who is trying to put over some community organization, everyone who is trying to do anything is selling something.

In our business, in our homes, and in our social relations, whether we realize it or not, we often fail to inspire confidence in our proposals for the simple reason that we have not given sufficient thought to the preparation of our case.

Meanwhile, lost jobs, divorces, personal feuds, ruined reputations, lost causes—failures of worthwhile ventures of all kinds—occur for the simple reason that we contribute to the mistaken thinking of others by neglecting to give them full information.

I know a case where a man was fired because he failed to keep his boss informed about a personal matter. This salesman had for several months been turning in reports that had errors in them. The general sales manager, noticing these errors week after week, came to the conclusion that the salesman was getting careless. Maybe he was drunk half the time. How else could he turn in reports with such obvious errors?

An order was passed along to the sales supervisor to discharge the man. It wasn't until three months later that the sales supervisor learned that this salesman had been gradually going blind, that he feared to tell anyone about it, that he had been dictating his reports to a public stenographer who knew nothing about the business and who was therefore unable intelligently to check the reports before they were turned in, and that the man himself was unable to read them because of his failing eyesight. When these facts came to light and were called to the attention of the general sales manager, he felt pretty bad about the whole situation, contacted the salesman whom he had fired, saw to it that he got the best medical care possible, and reinstated him on the payroll.

I know of one outstanding executive who delegates to his right-hand man the job of keeping him informed on all kinds of personal matters of his staff. This executive knows when a man's wife is in the hospital, when a new baby is born, when a man is having wife or sweetheart trouble, when he is under medical care, when he is taking night school courses, or when there is jealousy or friction or collusion among members of his staff. He makes an honest effort to keep himself well informed, not only on the work angles but on the human, personal angles of everyone who works for him, simply to protect himself against the possibility of jumping at mistaken judgments on the basis of inadequate information.

But so long as most executives fail to do this, any employee interested in gradually acquiring the confidence of his boss should devise some means for keeping his employer well informed.

Some employers are making the belated discovery that it is up to them to keep their workers reasonably well informed about the various factors that influence their business, if they are to gain and to hold the confidence of their employees. Simple, easy-to-read, easy-to-understand annual reports are just as interesting to the workers as they are to the stockholders. An explanation of the outside factors that may affect the business in the days to come—factors over which the company has no control—helps the worker to understand the true reasons for changes in wage rates, temporary layoffs, or any other conditions of employment that are of vital interest to him.

Some companies send letters to each worker's home; others have well-edited company publications; still others conduct periodic meetings at which the leading representatives of management keep the workers informed concerning what is going on and encourage them to ask questions.

I asked a brilliant attorney, "How do you explain the fact that you win such a high percentage of your cases?"

"It's because my opponents are too lazy to prepare their cases," he replied.

Two of the best friends I have lost confidence in each other and were divorced, and the hearts of their children were torn, solely because neither of them took the initiative in time—while their minds were still open—to enter into a full discussion of their mutual errors and desires.

In my own business experience, I have proved over and over again that any salesman can quickly increase his income if he will first open the prospect's mind, second, select an appropriate time as early as possible and present a complete statement of his case to fit that prospect's interests, and third, ask for the order. Many salesmen fail because they never get over their complete story, which is the only sound basis for gaining the prospect's confidence and asking for the order.

So don't forget that once you've opened a mind, your best bet for winning and holding the confidence of others is to inform them fully in the beginning, and to continue to keep them posted with a reasonably complete statement of your case.

However, in preparing a *reasonably* complete statement of your case, be sure that you don't bore the listener.

THINK IT THROUGH, KEEP IT BRIEF, MAKE IT INTERESTING

The importance of the case dictates the length of your presentation. Obviously, you shouldn't take more than a few minutes to effect a minor sale or ask a minor favor. And even though you're trying to put over a deal that runs into the millions or settle a matter that affects the lives of a nation, you'd better not count on sustained attention for more than an hour at a time. In fact, if you've been reading this book for over an hour, you'd better put it aside for a while. P. S. But don't forget to pick it up again.

In every instance, your case should be thought out in advance, it should be kept as brief as possible, and it should be made as interesting and palatable as you can make it—eliminating all boresome details.

You know how impatient you get when someone rambles on and on without any terminal facilities and insists on boring you with a lot of detail that does not interest you in the least. It's a common experience with all of us. It happened to me one day when I tried to buy a plant for my wife's birthday.

Inquiring about the prices of gardenia plants at a Southern California nursery, I told the oriental flower fancier who owned the establishment that his prices seemed high.

"Peepee don' know," he complained repeatedly, as he launched into what threatened to be a lengthy discourse on the gardenia. I tried to interrupt him, but his enthusiasm had gained too much momentum. Now he was reveling in the long and arduous tasks of conceiving a gardenia, nursing it and fondling it through its infant trials, guarding and encouraging its early childhood—tasks successfully performed only by the most skillful hands, informed by years of study and guided by the intuitions of countless generations of ancestors who also raised the gardenia—until the gardenia plant became sturdy enough to be sold safely to an amateur gardener.

The only thread in his conversation that held my interest was his continual repetition of "Peepee don' know." After a while it suddenly dawned on me that what he meant was "People don't know." Then I was ready to leave. After all, I had neither the time nor the inclination to take a course on gardenia raising. I only wanted a gardenia. I didn't care particularly where gardenias came from. I just thought that a gardenia plant would please my wife, look nice in her garden, and maybe impress the neighbors. That's all

This complaint that "people don't know," however, is not confined to the flower fancier. I seem to find it at every hand.

Not long ago I attended a conference in which a brilliant young inventor explained his latest brain child to some financiers. Their minds were open. They had asked for the meeting. It was an important meeting for this young inventor. It was his big chance. The men he was talking to had the money and the connections to put his invention over.

We arrived at his workshop shortly before noon. The inventor began by dwelling on the exhilarating conception, the painful birth, and the expensive development of his big idea. From there he went on and on with endless figures and charts.

At ten minutes after two, one of the financiers exploded.

"Look!" he interrupted the inventor. "We've been listening to you for over two hours. You've led us into the jungle of your scientific adventures, pointing out every difficulty—every single dark cave you've gotten yourself into and you've explained in detail how you finally fought your way out. And we're still not out of the woods. I *still* don't know what you've got or what it'll do for *me!*"

"I'm coming to that," assured the inventor. "But you men don't know what I've been through."

"Look," the financier interrupted again. "People are not interested in processes. People are interested in results. People will never know what 'you've been through.' People don't care. That's the secret cross you'll have to bear alone. People don't give a hoot how difficult it was for you to arrive at something worth while. They want to know what it will do for *them*."

Believe me, my sympathies were with the inventor but I couldn't help feeling that old Mr. Moneybags was right.

Another time I was seated in a sales manager's office when one of his salesmen walked in.

"How did you make out?" asked the sales manager.

"Well, I'll tell you," began the salesman. "I went down there right after lunch and was standing in the reception room when . . ."

"Wait a minute," interrupted the boss. "Did you get the order?"

"Well, what I was going to say is—he wouldn't see me at first. I tried for two solid hours to . . ."

"Joe! What do I care whether you *tried hard* or not? What I want to know is 'Did you get the order?' "

People will never know what "Joe" goes through to get an order—except his wife, and she probably wishes she didn't.

When Mrs. Brady calls up Mrs. Broody to welcome her back from the hospital and invite her to play bridge, she doesn't want to hear all about the gruesome operation; she just wants to know, "Can you play or can't you?"

Recently I heard of a child's book review which read, "This book tells more about penguins than I am interested in knowing."

It reminded me that we are always in danger of telling others more about ourselves than they are interested in knowing.

People don't want to know what you and I have been through.

So let's not expect them to.

When you build up a reasonably complete statement of your case, give your listener the main payoff in the headline, develop it only as far as you have to, and pass up all the boresome detail.

The world is overrun with "inventors" and "reformers" and people with "great ideas," who are forever babbling about better ways of doing things, but who never gain the confidence, even of their open-minded friends, because they never quite get around to the point of actually working out a practical and comprehensive presentation of their ideas.

There's one good reason for this. On this score, I have had more trouble with myself than with anyone I know. Perhaps you have noted that whenever you get an idea, that idea is invariably accompanied with a burst of enthusiasm, and your initial inclination is to bounce right off your chair and go and tell someone about it. This has certainly happened to me often enough. And before you are halfway through telling the other fellow about your great idea, he interrupts with a lot of plain and fancy objections that make you feel like an imbecile for ever thinking of such a thing.

And if the objections raised are valid, you feel like kicking yourself for not having thought of these things first so that you could save yourself the embarrassment of suggesting an idea that had so many holes in it. And a lot of our ideas are like that.

But even though your idea is a sound one, you get into all kinds of trouble by talking it over prematurely with others. Because you haven't thought your idea through, you are unable to anticipate and to answer the questions and objections raised by others. The energy created by the idea is dissipated in premature conversation with others who throw cold water on your plans and paint pictures of mountainous difficulties that make you afraid.

If, on the other hand, when you get an idea you keep it to yourself, the energy created by the idea will force you to think it through and will sustain you in anticipating and surmounting the objections and difficulties involved.

One of the most difficult things in the world is to keep an idea to yourself until it is fully flowered and developed. But it is necessary to do this if you are to be successful in developing a reasonably complete statement of your case that will gain the confidence of others. Anyone who falls into the natural tendency of shooting off half cocked every time he gets an idea soon acquires the reputation of being a fellow with a lot of crazy ideas that never pan out, and you can't gain confidence that way.

I don't mean to contend that it is impossible to get help from anyone else in the development of your ideas, but I do mean that the time to discuss your idea with anyone is *after* you have thoroughly thought it through yourself, and even then your discussions should be confined to those who are in an authoritative position to offer suggestions that are really worth while.

DON'T MAKE OVERENTHUSIASTIC PROMISES

In building up a strong case that will win the confidence of others, it is so easy to let our enthusiasm run away with us, and to make promises that are not easy to fulfill.

But the master salesman, and the master in human relations, practices and knows the tremendous value of *under*statement instead of *over*statement. He knows that conservative promises immediately gain the confidence of the more intelligent, and he knows that conservative promises are easier to fulfill, not only for the more intelligent but also for the less intelligent—thereby building the long-range confidence of both.

When I was in the Navy during World War I, our chief petty officer approached me one afternoon. I was open-minded to the chief, because, after all, he was the boss. He asked me to go out on a date with him that night, and he built a glowing picture of the "lovely sister" his date would bring along.

That night this lovely sister turned out to be "Mamie with the thick glasses." My confidence in the chief was shattered. In fact, from then on my mind was closed whenever the chief talked about dates.

A mother promised her high-school daughter, Mary, that she would give her $500 on her twenty-first birthday if she wouldn't smoke a cigarette until she was twenty-one. Mary didn't. But when her twenty-first birthday came along, her mother didn't have the $500.

A salesman promised his boss that he would land a big order by the first of the year. When January rolled around, he didn't have the order.

A research director promised the president of the company that he would have a report finished by Tuesday—sure. But when Tuesday came, he found that the information needed for his report wasn't in yet.

If an employer tells you you can make $200 a week within a year, and you only make $87, and furthermore you learn that no salesman in the history of the business ever averaged $200 a week, you lose confidence in that employer.

I know a young man who made a terrific first impression on a prospective employer and landed a good job on the basis of his sales talk. But after he got the job, the boss found out that this young man lacked the ability to get along with others in the organization and acted as if he were "too good" to perform some of the routine tasks required. So the boss lost confidence in this young man and discharged him.

It's a temptation to take advantage of the other person's ignorance and make exaggerated promises. But when the evidence catches up with you, you pay a heavy price in the lost confidence of that person.

All of us make careless promises that we don't have to make at all. We don't have to "promise the moon" in order to get a person's confidence. In fact, we ultimately lose the confidence we are trying to build up with these very promises with which we hope to gain it.

One of the wisest teachers I ever had told me, "Never make an unqualified promise about the future."

Certainly it is vital in all our human relations to see to it that any promise we do make really comes true.

AVOID THE CONTROVERSIAL ATTITUDE

We are indebted to Myron Colbert for this:

> In controversial moments, my perception's rather fine,
> I always see both points of view . . . the one that's
> wrong and mine.

No matter how right you are, no matter how wrong the other fellow is, and no matter how much evidence you have to prove it, you seldom gain his confidence by trying to argue him down.

It's an old adage that the best way to win an argument is to avoid it entirely. For argument closes a mind.

When you set out to *prove* something, it's perfectly natural for the other person to think up all the reasons why he shouldn't do as you say.

But when you put your ideas in the form of a suggestion, based on a fair and complete appraisal of both sides, his interests and your interests, you arouse no antagonism. The other fellow may still do as he pleases and he'll be more likely to do as you wish so long as he knows he can do as he pleases.

No one likes to be forced into doing anything—even for his own good.

If your suggestion is sound, you can well afford to admit that it has its weaknesses—in fact, your presentation of the weak points along with the strong points builds real confidence, for any intelligent person can see that there are no "perfect" answers to any problem. Anyone can always think up a good reason against doing anything, so why arouse him?

How many times have you heard parents argue with their children and close their minds about going to bed or going to Sunday school?

Even a child is quite able to look at both sides of such a question, and any parent will be more successful in gaining his child's confidence if he openly presents both sides.

For instance, one elementary school youngster of Winfield, Kansas, is reported as having summarized the reasons for and against attending Sunday school, as follows:

"Reasons for Going—It is the Christian thing to do. It will do me some good. It pleases Grandfather.

"Reasons for Not Going—I like to sleep on Sunday morning. The preacher bores me. My Sunday pants scratch."

D. B. Taylor, able writer for *Printers' Ink,* is responsible for a "tabloid study showing how ten types of salesmen handle things when the buyer puts on fighting clothes." In this study, Mr. Taylor gives the following description of the type of salesman whom he calls "the diplomat."

The diplomat had an uncanny ability of quickly inserting himself into an argument on the side of the customer, while still effectively representing his house.

He would march into the roaring customer's office and that surprised individual would suddenly find a sincere and valuable ally instead of an antagonist.

The knowledge that he had a rare talent for soothing customers led the diplomat into all manner of impossible situations. The diplomat deliberately welcomed jams. He found that his successful adjustment of these difficulties actually welded the customer firmly to him in an almost childish faith in the diplomat's ability to serve his interests intelligently.

Men and women who use this kind of diplomacy collect large rewards not only in business; they enjoy the rewards of confidence wherever they go.

HOW WE LOSE CONFIDENCE IN UNGUARDED MOMENTS

Every rule we've given so far about winning the confidence of others is recognized on sight as being of fundamental importance. And when the big business conference is held at the office, or when a major question arises at home, or when you're after anything that means a lot to you, you are likely to be on the alert and to remember to use these rules.

But all of us have our unguarded moments—when nothing "big" is at stake—moments when we forget to use what we know, moments when we make careless statements and perform thoughtless acts which are unworthy of us. Yes, moments when we revert to type and even forget to act like a lady or like a gentleman.

And it's in these unguarded moments that we can lose a heap of confidence that might have taken months or years to build up.

Over the Christmas holidays, for instance, I saw a striking example of how a little, unimportant occasion was sufficient to weaken a high confidence relationship between a rising young sales executive and his boss.

The company was having a Christmas party. The main work for the year was done. Everyone was in the holiday spirit. The boss himself was serving cocktails. This young sales executive felt like relaxing. It seemed like the time to relax. And it was. But this fellow overdid it.

Several days late῀ he came to me and said. "Boy, did *I* have myself a time at that Christmas party! I didn't even know what went on after six o'clock. The fellows have been telling me how I acted, and I don't think the boss liked it very much, do you?"

"Why? Has the boss said anything to you?" I asked.

"Well, he hasn't *said* anything to me, but when I saw him this morning, there was a chilly formality about him that I've never felt before. And I can feel it in my bones that the way I behaved at the Christmas party has something to do with it. But after all, it was *he* who kept offering me another cocktail and when the boss himself offers to pour you another drink, how can you possibly turn it down?"

Now there's a common occurrence. Perhaps you've faced the situation where the host offered another drink, you really didn't want to take another one, or you felt you shouldn't, but you didn't want to act like a prude so you went along with the rest to be a good sport.

I'm indebted to a good friend of mine for the answer to this one.

At another company celebration, following a strenuous annual sales meeting, I was one of those who had the honor of pouring the cocktails.

When I kept "insisting" that this friend let me pour him another, he said, "Look, Doc, you want me to *enjoy* myself, don't you?"

"Of course," was my quick comeback. "Is there anything I can do?"

"Yes," he said, "*don't* pour me another cocktail because I don't believe I'd *enjoy* another drink. I'm feeling swell right now. I've had just enough."

That made a deep impression on me and helped me to understand why this man enjoys such solid confidence among his friends and associates.

After all, we know that it is part of the duties of a host to see that his guests are well served and enjoy themselves. Offering another helping of turkey or another drink is a courtesy. We don't have to take the host's "insistence" at face value, and the person who does is likely to wind up with the reputation of being a glutton or a drunkard.

We all know people like that. The morning after the celebration I just told you about, I overheard the following conversation in the men's room between "two of the boys."

"How d'ya feel, Eddie?"

"Okay, Tommy—and you?"

"I feel all right. But geez, didn't Joe make a fool of himself?"

Yes, at every party or celebration where there's "drinking," it seems that there's always one person who makes a fool of himself. The important point for us is to be sure that we are never that person.

Some people can "hold their liquor" and others can't.

Some shouldn't drink at all; liquor makes them less attractive, emphasizes their weaknesses, loosens a crude or nasty tongue, makes them "over-sexy," makes them want to fight, makes them ill.

With others, a drink or two seems to make them more attractive. Liquor relaxes them. Their conversation improves, they are more polite and engaging. I don't believe in "prohibition," and I don't believe there is any set rule that applies to everyone. It's a personal problem. Everyone should know how liquor affects *him*. Then he should stay on the safe side—for his own good and for the good of his impression on others—and any time he finds himself unequal to that task, he should let liquor alone entirely.

All of which may sound obvious, but you know and I know that, when it comes to "drinking," the obvious is often overlooked—sometimes completely undermining the confidence of others.

Not long ago, an able executive told me of a business friendship which he had developed over a period of years with one of the leaders in his line.

"This man was all ready to invite me to join his business," said the executive. "I held a dinner party and invited him and his wife as guests of honor. At that dinner party, I made the mistake of taking one drink too many, and in one evening destroyed all the confidence I had built in five years. I have never seen my friend since that night."

Someone has said that the most important thing about liquor is that it should never become important.

Of course, there are other ways in which we may lose confidence in unguarded moments.

"One dirty joke was enough to shatter my confidence in that man," a business associate told me. "He was at our home for dinner and during the after-dinner conversation, he told a story that embarrassed a few of the ladies. It's not that I'm fussy about such things, but it showed poor judgment and bad taste. Now, I have less confidence in his business judgment in general."

The effect of any story should be anticipated in terms of our audience. As you know, a story that might be perfectly acceptable among a group of men or even a group of women, can reflect poor judgment in a mixed group of both men and women. Some stories that are acceptable in an adult audience should never be told when children or adolescents are present.

It's a natural inclination in all kinds of storytelling bees to permit ourselves to be lured into the common error of "going the other fellow one better." Someone invariably starts the ball rolling by telling a story that's just a "teensy-weensy" bit off color, and things go from bad to worse until someone winds up with a story that everyone wishes he hadn't told.

A story has to be a good story to help you; and it doesn't have to be far off color to hurt you.

When in doubt, don't tell it.

Another way we lose confidence in unguarded moments is by making careless statements that we don't even believe ourselves.

On a cross-town bus, I saw a little boy about five, point to the library building at 42nd Street and Fifth Avenue, and ask his father,

"Is that your office, Daddy?"

"No, that's a library," was his father's curt reply.

"What's in a library?" asked the boy.

"Books."

"What does it say in books?"

"It says to mind your Daddy. Now shut up."

You know the kind of questions children ask.

"What kind of a tree is that, Daddy?"

"Is that the biggest ship in the world, Daddy?"

'Daddy, where's that airplane going?"

"When's our dog going to have babies, Daddy?"

These are serious questions to a child, and any parent who habitually brushes them off with careless answers— answers that he doesn't even believe himself—is in a fair way to lose the confidence of his child. For when the child gets a little older, and finds that his father was so often wrong, you can hardly expect him to accept with complete confidence other statements, however wise, that his father may make.

It's only reasonable to expect that any fair-minded child, after learning that his father's answers don't square with the teacher's, will soon think to himself, "Gee, the old man must be slipping."

One morning an insurance salesman called me over the phone from the reception room.

"I'm not going to try to sell you any insurance. All I want is ten minutes of your time to explain a brand new policy that our company developed especially for men like you."

I opened my mind to this fellow, but when he got into my office, he *did* try to sell me some insurance, he *didn't* leave in ten minutes, and the brand new policy that his company offered *wasn't* developed especially for a man like me.

Obviously, we can't gain anyone's confidence with careless statements that we don't even believe ourselves.

You can win the confidence of others and enjoy all its benefits if you will think of the other fellow's interests as well as your own, select the right time to present your evidence, give the other fellow a reasonably complete statement of your case, make your promises come true, avoid a controversial attitude, and guard against the thoughtless acts and careless statements which are unworthy of you.

CHAPTER V

Inspiring Belief

Confidence, if consistently cultured and nurtured with favorable evidence, ultimately flowers into sound belief. Once you've gained a person's confidence, your next job is to keep on showing him, in every *new* situation that arises, that you are worthy of his belief in you. And that's Step No. 3 in persuading him to believe what you say and do what you want: (See Exhibit III.)

A belief relationship represents the highest plane of human relations. To believe in one another is not only the most civilized, most satisfying, and most beautiful form of human relationship, it is the most efficient. It saves so much time.

HOW OTHER PEOPLE FEEL ABOUT YOU

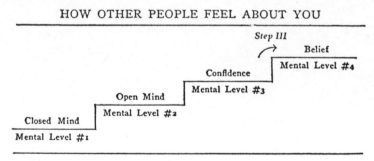

EXHIBIT III

You can easily see why. The person who is merely open-minded requires complete proof before he will do as you ask, while even the person who has confidence in you requires some. But as his confidence in you grows, he requires less and less proof before he follows your recommendations, and when a person believes in you, he does what you ask without question—without delay.

ARE BELIEF RELATIONSHIPS TOO IDEALISTIC?

I've never talked with anyone yet who doesn't agree that a belief relationship is a wonderful thing. But nearly everyone seems to think that—like perfect love—it's entirely too idealistic to be realistic.

They don't quarrel with the fact that it is a desirable form of human relationship, or that it's efficient, or that it saves time, or that it is most satisfying. Their only contention seems to be that it is almost unattainable and that rarely is a person worthy of the implicit trust that goes with a belief relationship.

And I agree that it is rare to find anyone who honestly deserves your wholehearted belief in relation to any kind or every kind of a life situation which may arise.

The moment we begin to think about belief relationships, we must immediately recognize that no one believes in anyone in relation to *everything*, barring exceptional cases, unless he has intelligently tried to achieve such high relationships.

But it's common to find one person believing in another person implicitly in connection with some one thing.

An office manager says, "You never have to double-check that fellow. When he gives you a set of figures, they're right."

An heiress says, "Tommy's the greatest chauffeur in the world, we think. He's been with us for years."

A salesmanager says, "He's our top salesman. I have complete faith in his ability to handle any prospect."

A housewife says, "We'll never starve. Donald has come through every business depression yet with flying colors. Conditions just can't get tough enough to lick him."

A clerk says, "When it comes to insurance, I put everything

in his hands and follow his judgment without question. He knows exactly what I need."

The chairman of the board of a large business enterprise says to the new president, "From now on, Harry, it's your business to run your way. Any decisions you make, however far-reaching, are okay with me. If I can ever help you, call on me. But you'll have no interference from me whatsoever in running this show, because I and all the rest of the stockholders have supreme confidence in you."

A daughter says, "There'll never be another cook like Mother."

A father says, "Bill's a real student. He doesn't need any pressure from me. I have no doubt in my mind at all that he will get through that engineering course. In fact, he might cop some honors."

And every now and then, you have the high privilege of knowing a person who deserves your wholehearted belief in every possible kind of situation of any importance—a person whom you have seen conduct himself with poise, control, and good judgment in all kinds of personal, social, and business situations—a person wise enough not to undertake anything that he is not able to accomplish—a straight thinker, a planner, a man of action with broad vision, deep human sympathies, and sound beliefs, a man who senses the consequences of his actions far into the future, a man you would trust with your pocketbook, your wife, your daughter, your all.

Yes, it's rare, but it can happen.

I know several such people. One of these men is a former boss of mine. Another is a fellow I went to school with. Another is my favorite teacher, who has counseled me repeatedly since I left school. Another is a fraternity brother of mine. Another is a business associate.

Naturally, there are certain family belief relationships which I could add.

I don't mean for one minute that these people represent perfection. They don't have to be perfect to deserve my belief in them. Minor mistakes that they may make are of no consequence to me. And when it comes to important matters, I believe the judgment of these people is either equal or superior to mine, and that any mistakes that they might make in important matters are mistakes that I might well make myself.

One of the best tests that anyone can apply to himself is to put down on paper the names of those who believe in him. Try this yourself. Then put down the names of those in whom *you* believe. You needn't be surprised to find the same names on both lists, for your own capacity for belief in others is what determines whether others believe in you.

If you cannot honestly say to yourself that you enjoy such a relationship with one or more persons, you can safely conclude to yourself, privately, that you still have some work to do with yourself in developing your own capacity for belief in others, and until you yourself attain this capacity for belief in others, obviously you cannot hope to inspire others to believe in you.

Naturally, the number of people who deserve your wholehearted belief in any and every possible kind of situation will be relatively few, because those who have such outstanding and well-rounded ability are always exceptional.

With all of my conscious efforts to build belief relationships with as many people as possible, I have been successful in developing such *complete* belief relationships in only a limited number of instances.

But there are literally hundreds of people with whom I enjoy *partial* belief relationships through first-hand experience. I believe in their ability as good doctors, lawyers, executives, inventors, musicians, entertainers, administrators, educators, builders, mechanics, dentists, writers, artists, production men, financiers, statesmen, butchers, grocers, bakers, candlestickmakers, and what not—people I've worked for, people who have worked for me, people who have served or counseled me, people I've served or counseled, people who have given me plenty of real, tangible evidence to show that they deserved my belief in relation to this one phase of their life.

And, in addition to all these, there are literally thousands of people whom I have never even met, but in whom I believe implicitly as far as the performance of a specific task is concerned. Every time I board an airplane I believe in the pilot—I put my very life into the hands of this man I've never met. Whenever I get into an elevator, I automatically express a belief in those who have built and inspected, and in the man who runs, that elevator. Every time I eat in a restaurant, or even at home, I show my belief in the manufacturers and processors of the food I eat.

Whenever I drive my car, I believe in the hundreds of people and in the many organizations responsible for the various parts of that automobile.

But going beyond these cases within my own experience that affect my day-to-day existence, I believe, and I think you do, in the fundamental goodness of men everywhere.

Now that takes in a lot of territory. But I believe that most men, wherever you find them, are fair. I believe their hearts are in the right place. I believe they are capable of reasoning. I believe they have a lot to learn about the use of reason, but I believe that if, as, and when they are taught how to think, as well as how to feel, they will make fewer mistakes, lose much of their shortsightedness, and become more interested in helping instead of fighting and killing each other.

I believe that anyone who sets out to do it can prove to man that it really pays him to learn more about and to abide by the laws of human nature.

I believe that anyone who knows these laws immediately

begins to look upon the open mind as a prime necessity if people are to live and learn and progress and to associate productively with each other.

I believe that the average person anywhere can be persuaded, providing enough evidence is given him, that confidence and belief relationships with others should be planned and extended to anyone who deserves such trust, for the simple reason that such relationships provide the basis for the most efficient, the most productive, and the most satisfying way of life.

I believe that any normal person can be convinced that honesty is merely another form of common sense, that a person who steals is stupid, that even the selfish person, who really doesn't care about anybody else, cannot safely acquire and retain the things he wants for himself without delivering something to others in return for what he wants. And once a person gets interested in serving others in return for what he wants, he soon learns that he gets a bigger kick out of giving than out of getting.

I believe that by this process—a process that can be speeded up enormously with the proper education and leadership— man will ultimately discover for himself that some form of human service is the only path to real happiness.

It is this fundamental belief in man that motivates me every day in the work that I do. If I didn't have this belief, I certainly wouldn't be running an educational project.

It is this fundamental belief in man that convinces me that man, all over the world, will readily embrace a free and democratic way of life any time it is offered to him under the proper leadership and training, and that the United States of America, because of its background and its progress in this direction, is admirably fitted to provide this leadership and training.

You can see, then, how my belief relationships with people

guide my whole life. And it's the same way with you.

Belief relationships are available to anyone. And the extent to which he develops them is limited solely by his own capacity for belief.

Unfortunately, however, you know, as well as I know, that most people do not *think* in terms of a belief relationship with anybody in relation to anything.

And because they do not think in terms of achieving belief relationships with others, they never attain such relationships, even among those who are fully deserving.

Furthermore, without any conscious effort or plan to improve their relations with others, they are continually in the process of tearing down the confidence and destroying even the open-minded relationships that they temporarily enjoy.

The result is that they believe in no one and no one believes in them.

No wonder most people never get anywhere in their human relationships at home, in business, or any place else.

In business, for example, you know the type of fellow who does not believe that anyone else is capable of performing a job as well as he can. The fellow who's continually checking and double-checking and hounding the other fellow the moment he gives him a job to do. The fellow who is always squawking that he cannot get anyone who's reliable or accurate or trustworthy. The fellow who has to do everything for himself. Such a man never rises to an executive position because he can't be happy delegating work to others.

I know the head of a small business who will never have a real organization of any proportions. His business will always be a "one-man band." Its growth will always be restricted within the limits of his own personal service, for the simple reason that this man does not trust anyone in his employ to the extent that he will give him a job to do and let him alone. And in this type of operation, he cannot attract top men to help him. His own mistrust is responsible for the fact that the only ones willing to work for him are second-raters. Men like this always remain "small" whether they are in business for themselves or employed in a large organization.

The greatest business leaders of all time, including Carnegie and Schwab and innumerable others, have admitted that their success was attributable primarily to the fact that they surrounded themselves with men who were smarter than they were—men they believed in. Now these great industrial leaders naturally made many mistakes in the selection of men. Some of the men they hired were unequal to the trust given them. But that did not stop these leaders from having the *capacity* of believing in others, and this sustained capacity is what carried them to leadership.

In the home, the wife who is continually checking and double-checking and cross-questioning her husband concerning his motives, his work, and where he has been every minute of the time on his night off gradually destroys any confidence or belief relationship with her husband through her own suspicious attitude. And the same goes for the double-checking husband.

. Wherever you go, you find people who are so cynical and suspicious that they "don't trust nobody." And their own distrust—their own lack of capacity for believing in others— promotes the distrust of others in all their family, business, and social relations.

On the other hand, those most loved, most respected, and most successful, as parents, friends, associates, and leaders, are invariably those who have the capacity for believing in others and who show it.

People want to believe in you. They would rather *believe* you are right than to have you try to *prove* you are right, because it makes it easier for them. People don't want to have to exert themselves to examine and analyze everything you say to find out whether there are any loopholes or selfish motives. Ever since the dawn of human consciousness, man has yearned for something, someone, he could *believe* in.

People want you to believe in them. Yes, the greatest prize you can offer anyone is your belief in him. He wants it more than money, more than power, more than glory. He needs the belief of others to give him *self*-respect. You give a man your belief, your wholehearted belief, your unqualified belief, your no-strings-attached belief, and he will rarely let you down. When you believe in a person, it is practically impossible for him to bring himself to the point of returning your trust with meanness or treachery or deceit. For in doing so he would lose his self-respect.

Getting right down to cases, whenever you feel that you have gained a person's confidence and have demonstrated repeatedly, as new situations arise, that you are worthy of his belief, you still have one final act to perform in order to inspire his belief in you.

ASK THE PERSON TO BELIEVE IN YOU

You must *ask* that person to believe in you—not in so many words, because words aren't enough, and they may prove embarrassing. For example, you could ask a person "Will you believe in me?" and he could say "Yes," and your relationship still wouldn't mean anything until it came to a test.

Here's the test of a belief relationship. Whenever you feel that a person is ready to believe in you, just ask him to do something of some importance without giving him evidence to prove why he should do it.

For instance, one day at my hotel in Chicago, I had a long-distance telephone call from the president of a large organization who had retained me to work on some of their marketing problems. He told me he had to select a man for an important executive position with his company and wanted to know whether I could recommend anyone.

I knew I had this executive's confidence. I had already given him plenty of evidence. Now, I wanted to move him into a belief relationship.

So instead of giving him my candidate's name and telling him all the reasons why I felt he should select this man, I merely said, "Your problem is solved. I know the right man for the job."

"What's that?" he asked.

I repeated, "Your problem is solved. I know the right man for the job." Then I added, "Now we're talking long-distance. Is there anything else you want me to do?"

"Why . . . that's wonderful!" he said. Then he talked briefly about another matter he wanted me to take care of and concluded by saying, "If you're sure you have the right man, go ahead and get him as soon as possible."

If this executive had insisted on having some evidence as to who the man was, I'd have given it to him, and understood that I merely had his confidence. But when he didn't, this proved I had his belief. I found the right man in a branch office of this same organization, recommended him and he was appointed.

From that instant on, I never accompanied my recommendations to this chief executive with a lot of evidence. And I did what he asked, without question. In fact, whenever he offered "reasons," I would interrupt, saying, "If that's what you want, I'll do it. You don't have to take any of your valuable time explaining 'why' to me."

This saved both of us a lot of time and expense. And by showing my belief in him, I inspired and preserved his belief in me.

In fact, that's one of the best ways to inspire anyone's belief in you. Show him that you believe in him.

My belief relationship with another business executive dates from the day we had the following conversation:

"Can you be in Chicago next Monday morning?" he asked me.

"I'll be any place you say, any time," was my reply.

Even though his request made necessary a difficult change in my plans, and he knew it, I didn't ask him for a lot of reasons, and from that day on, he didn't ask me for any.

People are eager to show their belief in you if you deserve it, and if you will but ask them.

On one occasion, I invited nearly a hundred business and educational leaders in the city of New York to get up at the crack of dawn and attend a seven-o'clock breakfast. It was inspiring to have them accept my invitation to a man, and to show by their presence that they believed in the cause I represented.

No matter where you go, if you listen to what people say, you will find them unconsciously seeking the belief of others—and sometimes getting it.

A housewife phones the butcher.

"Can you get me a real nice turkey around twelve pounds?"

"Yes, Mrs. Jones, I'll get you a nice one."

"What kind are you going to get?" she asks.

"Leave it to me, Mrs. Jones. I've never sent you a poor turkey yet, have I?"

"All right," says Mrs. Jones. "I'll depend on you to pick me out a nice one as you always do."

Now the butcher asked for her belief by reminding her that he was worthy of it, and he got it.

I sat in an executive's office and heard him say to his wife over the phone, "I know you believe in my judgment in such matters, dear." Then she said something. Then he said, "Well, that's fine. You just leave it entirely in my hands."

After he hung up, he turned to me and said, "You see,

Reilly. That illustrates your idea of asking a person to believe in you when you deserve that belief. My wife just called to discuss a purchase of a Christmas present for a relative in California. You heard what I said. She feels quite relieved about the whole matter. This idea of asking the other person to believe in your judgment, has saved me a lot of time. I used to have all kinds of long-drawn-out, annoying telephone conversations and discussions, not only with my wife but with people in general."

Sooner or later, in the presentation of any kind of a selling talk, the time comes when the salesman should ask for the order. After he's opened the mind of a prospect, after he's given that prospect a reasonably complete statement of his case, he's ready to ask the prospect to believe in him and buy.

The whole trouble is that most salesmen seem to get gun-shy when that time comes. They keep on talking and the first thing you know they've talked themselves out of an order, or they just let the whole decision hang. I honestly believe that if more salesmen knew how to ask others to believe in them they would have less difficulty in asking for the order. Because asking for the order and asking someone to believe in you is one and the same thing.

The biggest order I ever closed in my life admirably illustrates the point. One of our salesmen had set up an appointment for me to present our proposition to the management staff of a large industrial organization.

Every man in this organization who was involved in the decision to buy or not to buy our services was present. (That's the thing that every salesman prays for.) As soon as the usual procedure of opening the minds of these men and going through a reasonably complete statement of our case was finished, I asked this management staff if they had any questions. After answering these questions, I asked them for an immediate decision.

"You have seen how we can step up the effectiveness of your advertising—PLENTY!" I told them. "You men know more about our services right now than you ever will know, until you buy. More than you'll know an hour from now. More than you'll know tomorrow. We all know the memory curve sweeps downward, and a week from now, you'll only be aware of a small part of what I've just told you. And another thing, you've got me right here to answer any further questions that you might have. In short, you are in a better informed position to reach a decision right now than you ever will be.

"By a decision, I mean a Yes or No. We're satisfied to have you make up your mind one way or the other right now. If our presence embarrasses any of your confidential discussions, we'll retire and return in an hour or two hours or three hours or as long as it takes you men to arrive at your decision. It's your job to make decisions for the good of your organization, so will you make this decision for you and for me *now?*"

The management staff agreed that they could probably make up their minds in an hour, and asked us to return.

The moment we stepped out of the conference room, our salesman looked at me with the most pained expression on his face. "My Lord, Reilly," he began, "that's a big order we're after. Don't you think you were a little rough with them? Gee, we could afford to give them all the time in the world to make up their minds! That's a big organization!"

"We've got a better chance to get that business right now than we ever will have. And that's always the time to rest your case and ask for the order," I replied.

During that hour of impatient waiting, our salesman almost had a nervous breakdown. But when we returned to the offices of this great industrial organization for our decision, the decision was "Yes."

When I returned to my New York office, I found on my desk a huge bunch of chrysanthemums with $100 bills pinned on them. My boss was a real master at asking people to believe in him.

I saw one of the greatest salesmen I know close a deal over the phone that meant $40,000 to him, with the simple statement, "Boy, can we save *you* fellows some mistakes!"

In every single instance I've given of a person asking someone else to believe in him, you immediately recognize that it was done with the use of a simple assurance statement.

Now the use of assurance statements is quite common. But the main trouble is that people often use assurances at the wrong time. If a perfect stranger approached you on the street and said, "I can show you how to make big money," that assurance would leave you absolutely cold. For the simple reason that that person had not opened your mind, he had not gained your confidence with a reasonably complete statement of his case, and you therefore were not ready to believe in him—not ready to accept his assurance.

The time to use an assurance statement is when a person is ready to believe in you, and when you have shown that person that you deserve his belief.

When this time comes, don't hesitate to ask him to believe in you, and remember that the way to ask him is with a simple assurance statement.

"Your problem is solved. I know the right man for the job."

"Leave it to me, Mrs. Jones. I've never sent you a poor turkey yet, have I?"

"Well, that's fine. You just leave it entirely in my hands."

"You have seen how we can step up the effectiveness of your advertising—PLENTY!"

"Boy, can we save *you* fellows some mistakes!"

These are just a few of the many ways you can ask people to believe in you, and if you are worthy of their belief, you will get it.

But remember this. Just because a person has high confidence in you and is prepared to believe in you in one kind of situation doesn't mean that you can assume that same confide.1ce in an entirely different situation.

The ravishing young heiress may believe implicitly in her tall, dark, and handsome chauffeur—as a chauffeur. But as for romance—her mind may be closed—in spite of all the popular movies and magazine stories.

Seriously, though, a business associate may believe you are a great "front man," but a poor executive. Your boss may believe in you as a great salesman, but he may think you're wasteful when he looks at your expense accounts.

The president of your company may think you're a great treasurer and budget balancer, but he may think you're insulting in your human relations.

Your sweetheart may believe you are a great lover, but a poor provider. Your wife may believe you're a great provider, but that you're losing your romantic steam.

A friend may trust you with every dollar he has, and yet if you asked him to go up with you in your new airplane, his mind might be closed.

Your children may believe you are the finest cook in the world, but they also may think you're fussy and old-fashioned when it comes to "having fun," or they may think you're a terrible housekeeper.

A man may even believe that you are capable of running a business for him, but he may not trust you with his wife or his daughter.

The point is simple enough. So simple that we often forget it.

While it is true that when a person has confidence or belief in you in one situation, he is more likely to be open-minded toward you in anything you undertake; yet it is a grave mistake for you to assume the belief, or even the confidence, of another in any situation before you have given that person the usual evidence that proves you *deserve* it.

Finally, remember this. Whenever you do enjoy the high privilege of a belief relationship with your wife, or your husband, or your sweetheart, or your children, or your parents, or your business associates, or your friends, don't unwittingly show any lack of belief in them by asking a lot of unnecessary searching questions concerning what they've done or plan to do, and don't endanger their belief in you with long and superfluous explanations proving the wisdom of what you've done or plan to do.

The quickest way in the world to destroy your belief relationship with others is to check up on them at every turn, and shadow their actions in everything they do.

Belief inspires belief and you must believe in others if you would have them believe in you.

You can enjoy almost anyone's belief in you, if you will first strive to deserve it, second, ask for it, and third, be careful not to destroy unwittingly your belief relationships with others by failing to show belief yourself.

CHAPTER VI

What Belief Relationships Mean to You

When someone believes in you, he serves you without question. But he not only offers you *his* services. He helps you mightily in all your relations with others. He helps you to open the minds, gain the confidence, and inspire the belief of an ever-increasing number of people, thereby speeding up the realization of your objectives no matter what they may be.

No matter how well informed you may become, no matter how much knowledge you acquire in your chosen field, it is well to remember that very few have ever accomplished much or gone far in any line of human endeavor without the assistance and cooperation of a great many people. Friends, relatives, employers, business associates, superiors, subordinates, customers, tradespeople, nearly everyone you contact, can speed or retard your journey toward your goal.

THE IMPORTANCE OF SPONSORSHIP

It's not only WHAT you know but also WHO has confidence or belief in you. You need both ability *and* sponsorship, for it is certainly true that "many a prairie flower blooms unseen," and there are many who hide their unsponsored light under a bushel.

Whatever progress you make toward your goal can be almost entirely credited to those who believe in you, beginning with your mother and ending with your last friend.

All you have to do is to remember how you landed your best jobs or recall how you first met your most valued and most interesting friends. Think of the most satisfactory experiences you've had, the clubs or associations or fraternal organizations you belong to, the sales you've made, or any other kind of successful relations with others, and you'll find, in nearly every case, that you were sponsored by someone who had confidence or belief in you.

Anyone knows that you get further faster in all human relations when you have good friends who are willing to vouch for you and give you the old build up.

You may have a lot on the ball, but if you have no sponsorship *within* your organization, you won't go very far. And if you have no sponsorship *outside* your organization, you won't get very many attractive job offers.

With strong sponsorship within your organization, you are just bound to advance more rapidly, and if you have plenty of sponsors outside your organization, you are certain to get interesting offers that may represent real advancement.

Any time you receive such unsolicited offers, you *improve* your trading position. But whenever a person is forced to change jobs by other than invitation, he usually *hurts* his trading position.

If you are a housewife, and have no sponsorship in your community, you will find yourself being left out of many interesting clubs and social activities.

The first job I ever got as a boy, carrying newspapers in Pittsburgh, was secured through the sponsorship of a boyhood friend. Ever since I got out of school, every single job I've held has been by invitation—an invitation that was entirely due to the sponsorship of others.

Not long ago I wanted free radio time for educational purposes for five successive nights on the biggest national network available. The sponsorship of an influential business leader opened the minds of those who could give it to me, the proper timing of a reasonably complete statement of my case proved that I deserved their confidence, and the further sponsorship of several business and educational leaders inspired their belief in my cause and I was given the time requested at no cost.

No doubt you are thinking of many instances in which sponsorship has helped you realize some objective or other. Everyone knows intuitively that it's better to have someone else say you're a great guy than for you to have to say it yourself.

HOW TO GET POWERFUL SPONSORSHIP

Whenever you plan to use sponsorship, however, it is well to recognize that the power of your sponsorship pattern depends on two main factors:

1. Your relationship with your sponsor.
2. Your sponsor's relationship with the person to be influenced.

Yet I've seen men in sales work attempt to "sponsor" their first call on a new prospect by mentioning the name of some mutual acquaintance, without stopping to consider that a mere acquaintance isn't a very good sponsor, and without taking the trouble to find out in advance just what relationship exists between this acquaintance and the prospect. Obviously, that's not using sponsorship intelligently at all.

We must be more thoughtful in our selection of sponsors.

If you select a sponsor who believes in you and who also enjoys a belief relationship with the person to be influenced, your sponsorship pattern has plenty of power.

Confidence relationships are sometimes sufficient to get the desired results. But if either of the two key relationships is no more than open-minded, or perhaps negative, your sponsorship pattern is too weak to do much good.

As soon as we realize that our potential use of sponsorship

is directly dependent upon the number of people who have confidence or belief in us, we are impressed anew with the desirability of achieving such relationships with as many people as possible.

No matter what your objectives are, as soon as you form the habit of planning the accomplishment of each objective by listing the names of those who might be able to help you achieve your purpose, this habit automatically provides you with the necessary stimulus to extend and to develop your human relations.

DON'T LOVE 'EM AND LEAVE 'EM

Time after time, in counseling men on the use of sponsorship in connection with their career objectives, I run into this situation. Men who have been out in the business world for five, ten, fifteen, or even twenty years, tell me that they cannot think of the names of any good potential sponsors. Invariably, this means to me that they have forgotten all about most of their former friends and business associates.

"Think of your former bosses," I tell them. "Think of the salesmen who have called on you in previous business connections. Think of previous business and social and educational contacts of all kinds. If you've lived right, certainly you must have some good friends among them. Perhaps you've neglected them. But if you set about doing it in the right way, you can revive most of these friendships."

Many people forget all about friends until they lose their job or meet some kind of crisis and need help . . . quick. Then it's a little late. We cannot suddenly manufacture belief relationships with people. We must gradually develop them and preserve them, as a regular planned part of our everyday lives, if we are to enjoy the timely benefits of such relationships.

"Yes," you say, "but how does one set about reviving these forgotten friendships?"

The answer that I often give to this question is that confidence and belief relationships invariably deepen and mature when aged in the wood of service and affection. After I get a man to list his former bosses, business associates, educational contacts, and friends, I then ask, in connection with each name on his list, "How long has it been since you have seen or written this man? How long has it been since you have served him in some way or other? Can't you think of some way in which you could possibly serve him?"

As soon as a man begins to think in terms of developing sponsorship, it becomes perfectly obvious to him that he can't "love 'em and leave 'em." He can see that whenever he leaves a job, it is just as important to preserve his good relations with his old boss as it is to develop good relations with his new one.

The man who sponsored me on my first job out of school has long since retired. He's getting along in years now and lives many miles away. But I still write to him and our friendship now is deeper than ever. Just a few weeks ago I wrote him on his birthday congratulating him on his life of service. He was unable to answer the letter, but his wife wrote, "You can never guess what your letters mean to him and me. This one was just what he needed, for he has been desperately ill and loving messages such as yours act like the best tonic."

Every Easter it warms my heart to have an Easter card from a struggling young man whom I've had the privilege of serving.

One of my prized possessions is a Thanksgiving Day letter from a former teacher of mine, in which he writes, "This seems to be a logical time to say that I am thankful for your friendship, including both its frequent tangible manifestations and its intangible but real values."

There are one hundred and one ways of serving others and there are one hundred and one ways of thanking others for the favors they do for you—all of which contributes toward the preservation and development of our human relations.

You show me a man who has held his old friends while making new ones, and I'll show you a person who has no fears for the future.

In counseling others on their career problems, I have found that the surest way to eliminate any man's fear of unemployment is to show him how to extend and strengthen his human relations to the point where there are always at least three men who are willing to buy his services—his present employer and two others.

Relieved of his fears, a man invariably does a better job for his present employer, and knowing the value of the sponsorship of his present employer, whether he continues to work for him or not, his behavior tends to make his present position even more secure.

The interesting thing, however, is this. When a person begins to assume a service attitude toward others for good business reasons, he soon learns that it's a lot of fun. After all, the one foolproof law of human relations is to give more than you get from anyone.

Yes, belief relationships give you ever-ascending joy and satisfaction as you preserve and cultivate them through the years.

Incidentally, Christmas is always a good time to write a personal letter to anyone who has ever sponsored you.

From a more immediate standpoint, it is always wise to keep your sponsor well informed as to your progress with the person to be influenced.

For instance, on one occasion, when I was after an important business contract, I asked a friend who believed in me and who had the confidence of the prospect, to act as my sponsor. Then immediately after my first meeting with the prospect, I addressed the following letter to my sponsor:

I have had a very cordial meeting with Mr.—since you were in New York, and our discussion seemed to move toward a most satisfactory conclusion.

I wanted you to know this for I feel deeply grateful to you for your generous sponsorship.

After I landed the contract, I addressed this second letter to my sponsor:

I know you will be glad to learn that I have recently signed up The Blank Company, since it was your own generous sponsorship which was entirely responsible for making this interesting opportunity available to me.

I am looking forward to seeing you again on your next visit to New York so that I may thank you personally.

I believe in this practice of sponsorship so strongly that I use it invariably unless the person to be influenced already believes in me. Then and then only will I go direct to that person.

In every other instance, I try to think of someone who either believes in me or at least has confidence in me, and who also has the confidence or belief of the person who can give me what I want.

Any person who enjoys belief or high confidence relations with a sufficient number of people will (if he practices planned and grateful use of these relationships) be carried to success on the willing shoulders of his sponsors.

PRACTICE THINKING THIS WAY

The more we practice sponsorship, the more we are likely to remember to use sponsorship—in time. In fact, the same thing goes for every one of the simple rules of living presented in the preceding chapters that show you how to get others to believe in you.

Let's assume that you know all these rules by heart. Let's assume that you remember that the one sure way to open a mind is by helping the other fellow to be right. Let's assume that you recall that the way to win the confidence of others and enjoy all its benefits is to think of the other fellow's interest as well as your own, select the right time to present your evidence, give the other fellow a reasonably complete statement of your case, keep your promises, avoid a controversial attitude, and guard against the careless statements and thoughtless acts which are unworthy of you.

Let's assume that you thoroughly understand that you can enjoy almost anyone's belief if you will first strive to deserve it, second, ask for it, and third, be careful not to destroy it unwittingly by failing to show belief yourself.

It isn't enough to *know* these things. It isn't what you *know* that counts. It's what you *think of—in time*. And the only way that you will ever master the daily application of these rules of living is by practicing them until they become part of your mental habits.

Merely to know these rules does not make you a master of human relations any more than a mere knowledge of the rules for playing golf makes you a master golfer.

"I know . . . I should have kept my left arm stiff," smiled a lovely young lady in a pink sweater and perfect golf attire who had just sliced a brand new ball into a scenic lake to the far right of the first tee.

"Yes, you know what I've taught you by heart," replied the club professional. "But you'd better go back to the practice tee and hit some old balls until these rules become part of your muscular habits."

A. Lawrence Lowell, one-time president of Harvard University, said, "There is only one thing which will really train the human mind, and that is the voluntary use of the mind by the man himself. You may aid him, you may guide him, you may suggest to him, and above all, you may inspire him; but the only thing worth having is that which he gets by his own exertions; and what he gets is proportionate to the effort he puts into it."

In other words, these rules of living will work for you if you work to master them.

No one ever became a master of human relations or anything else without plenty of practice.

One dark, misty Sunday morning at 5 A.M. an astonished brakeman in the St. Louis railroad yard heard the strains of a concerto floating out on the still air. Yes, some darn fool was playing a piano—maybe a drunk.

On investigation the brakeman approached a car on a siding. But just as he prepared to step aboard an attendant pressed his index finger to his lips and said, "Sh!—Mr. Paderewski is practicing."

Yes, Mr. Paderewski had a concert scheduled for that afternoon in St. Louis.

Every day of a scheduled concert, it was Paderewski's custom to get up at 5 A.M. to practice.

And Paderewski was good.

You'll get into the habit of saying the right thing at the right time in *all* your human relations as soon as you form the habit of "feeling right" toward other people, and the only way you can do this is to *practice* feeling that way.

First of all, rid your mind of any hidden hates or grudges.

Then go one step further, and practice helping the other fellow to be right.

Dare to be the first to show confidence and belief in others, not only because of what it does for them but for the sake of what it does . . . to you.

There is nothing in the world you deserve that you cannot have, providing a sufficient number of people believe in you. That's what belief relationships mean to you in a very practical and immediate sense. If you haven't already developed the confidence or belief of a "sufficient number of people," the best way to go about getting it is to reread the earlier chapters of this book and begin to practice what they teach day in and day out.

CHAPTER VII

The Three Conditions Which
Permit The Use of Force

Now that we have defined the four mental levels in all human relations and have seen how the principles of persuasion can be used to open closed minds, win the confidence of others, and inspire their belief, we are prepared to find out what place the use of force has in our human relations and to determine the three basic conditions under which we may consider the use of force with some degree of safety.

Almost everyone agrees that emergencies and conflicts arise when it becomes necessary to use force as a last resort, but relatively few seem to realize how many forms force can take, and few know or understand the basic conditions which permit the use of force.

In most people's minds, force is an ugly word. It is usually associated with a dictator or a bully. It often connotes violence or oppression.

And while it is true that the flagrant misuse of force is responsible for this view in most people's minds, the fact of the matter is that the use of force in human relations includes the exertion of *any* kind of influence or power against the will or the wish or the consent of any person or group of persons. And sometimes, force is used on a person or on a group of persons for their own good.

For example, on the sidewalk of a New York City street,

a small tow-headed boy bounces a bright red ball. Suddenly the ball shoots out between two parked cars and the boy dashes after it. The owner of one of the cars arrives just in time to snatch the boy from the path of an approaching truck. The boy kicks and scratches and screams, "Lemme go! I want my ball!"

After the truck roars past, knocking the ball sky-high, even the little boy understands that this man has saved him from a serious accident.

You would do the same thing as this man did, if you had the power to do it, wouldn't you? Of course you would. You would forcibly restrain this boy from being hurt.

"Yes," you say, "but that's an emergency."

And it is.

But you would use force in such an emergency, if you could, because you are right, there is no time for persuasion, and you have the power to prevent a possible disaster.

While it is true that, in most of our everyday relations with others, we are able to rely on persuasion, it is equally true that there are many kinds of emergencies which arise when you feel that you've got to use force, and quickly, in order to protect yourself, or your job, or your reputation, or some member of your family, or your home, or your business, or your property, or even your country, from immediate damage or destruction.

No intelligent person ever deliberately uses force in any kind of a human situation unless and until all possible efforts at persuasion have failed. Even then, he may not elect to use force. He may decide to run away or to surrender. For before anyone can be successful in the use of force, however justified, he must "have what it takes" to overpower his opponent.

Meanwhile, when we feel that our cause is just, our impatience often leads us to use force *before* we have employed all means of persuasion. And even when we do exhaust all means of persuasion, we sometimes blindly elect to use force when we haven't got the necessary power to win.

All of which leads us to a statement of the three fundamental conditions which must exist before anyone can consider the use of force with any degree of safety.

1. When you are right and the other fellow is wrong—not in your own eyes alone, but in view of the common good of all concerned.

2. When you have used all reasonable means for peaceful discussion and persuasion, and the time has come when you must act.

3. When you've "got what it takes" to force the other fellow to do what's right for his own good and for the good of all concerned.

In the chapters which follow, we shall see how these realistic conditions, which must precede the intelligent use of force, apply in actual practice in the various phases of our human relations—all the way from the home we live in to international affairs.

CHAPTER VIII

The Use of Force in the Home

Perhaps the one place, above all others, where we might reasonably expect to forgo all use of force and to rely entirely on persuasion is within the hallowed portals of our own homes. There our love is greatest for all concerned. There, if any place, we should be able to rely entirely on peaceful persuasion.

But let's face it. Even in the best regulated families, emergencies or conflicts do arise in which (1) the parent is right, (2) there is either no time for persuasion or all efforts at persuasion fail and the time comes to act, and (3) the parent represents the only adequate enforcement agency that can use force for the good of all concerned.

The most obvious case in which all parents are sometimes obliged to use force is when a child makes a sudden move in a wrong direction. For example, if your child reached for a hot stove or started toward the path of an approaching truck, you would use force in such an emergency to restrain him and to protect him (and then you would talk things over later on), because you were right, there was no time for persuasion, and you had what it took to prevent an accident.

Then there are other cases which arise when you are right, when all efforts at persuasion fail, and when the time comes to act for the child's own good.

SPANKING AND OTHER KINDS OF FORCE

Under these circumstances, there are many parents who feel that there is nothing like an old-fashioned spanking to straighten out an erring child. One of the most unusual cases along this line that has ever come to my attention is that of a young man aged 20 who was fined fifteen dollars for annoying girls who passed his home. The New York City judge addressed the youth's father who was in the court room: "You should take charge and administer proper chastisement." Whereupon the father, a two-hundred-pound construction worker, hauled off and floored his son with one blow!

One of the main troubles with belting or spanking, however, is that few fathers are two-hundred-pound construction workers, and the time comes, sooner or later, when your children grow up to be bigger or at least stronger than you are. I've often thought that this may be one of the subconscious reasons why some parents just don't believe in spanking. As the veteran stage performer Pat Rooney said, "My father knew how to bring up children. He only hit us in self-defense."

Seriously, though, spanking, at best, is a form of physical force which represents the last resort, even when children are small, and I hold no brief on the subject one way or the other. The only thing I know is that, in spite of all our efforts at persuasion in our home, every one of our three children, when small, was thoroughly spanked— once. But we never had to resort to spanking a second time, for, from then on, they seemed much more willing to reason things out with us.

However, there are some parents who, rightly or wrongly, do not believe in spanking a child under *any* circumstances. What to do then?

Well, parents who do not believe in spanking usually use some other kind of force to keep peace in the family—such as not letting a child go someplace or do something that he wants to do, or making him perform chores which he thoroughly hates or depriving him of something he especially wants, or just giving him the old-fashioned silent treatment.

Not long ago, a father came to me with this problem. His daughter, aged nine, suddenly was refusing to go to school because she was "sick" or "had a headache." But every schoolday morning around ten o'clock, she "felt better" and was able to play with her dolls and listen to the radio.

The mother had the family physician check up on the child but he could find nothing wrong. They even had the teacher to dinner one night. Both the mother and the father tried to "reason things out" with the child, but that didn't work. And one morning when her mother tried to pick the child up bodily and put her in the car to drive her to school, she hung on to the dining-room table leg and became so hysterical that the mother became frightened and gave up.

I suggested to this young father that apparently the time had come when some form of force had become necessary, and the simplest solution I could think of was to make it more disagreeable for this child to stay home than it would be to go to school.

It was arranged that the next time his daughter was "too sick to go to school," she would be put to bed with the explanation that if she's too sick to go to school, then she's too sick to be up and around and play, and so she will just have to stay in bed without any dolls or radio and with the shades drawn until she does feel well enough to go to school. Meanwhile, the family physician supplied some harmless but bad-tasting liquid with the suggestion that she be given a spoonful of this every two hours.

The child stuck it out for two whole days! But on the third day she "felt fine" and seemed eager to go off to school. In fact, the parents have experienced no further difficulty along these lines.

A neighbor's boy liked to play with matches. A lot of parents have trouble some time or another on this score. One day, the mother told me, she walked into the living room to find the drapes on fire. And on another occasion the davenport was smoking and before they could get that under control, the living-room rug had also been ruined.

The frantic parents had tried "everything." They had sent the boy to bed without his supper. They had kept him from going to the movies for a whole month. The father had spanked him. They had talked with him until they were blue in the face. But nothing worked. They still found him lighting matches in the house.

Then one evening, the parents went into a huddle. They realized that the situation had become so serious that it demanded some kind of drastic action, and they decided on a practical *demonstration* to drive the points home.

First of all, they drove the boy by a building which had recently been destroyed by fire. They told him that that's what their home would look like if it burned down. They explained how precious their home was to all of them. Then they told him they were going to show him what fire would do to something that was very precious to *him*. They selected three out of six wooden soldiers which the boy prized highly among his toys. Out on an open lot they had the boy build a fire and burn the three wooden soldiers. As his precious toys were destroyed, tears streamed down the boy's face. This all happened several years ago, but since that time the boy has shown no further desire to play with matches.

While it is true that, in every family, emergencies and conflicts arise when it becomes necessary to use some form of force to keep peace in the family, all parents are very much interested in reducing such distasteful incidents to a minimum, and there are two ways in which this goal can be accomplished.

ENCOURAGE YOUR CHILD TO THINK FOR HIMSELF

The first way to reduce emergencies and conflicts with your child is to challenge him to think things through on his own, for this gives him a chance to show how smart he is.

For example, in a Philadelphia grocery store, huge sacks of potatoes were piled high on the floor. A young mother, standing at the counter, perused her shopping list while her dear little boy of six tried to scale the wall of potatoes. The grocery clerk was getting more and more apprehensive, but all the mother did to relieve the situation was to swing her hand in the general direction of the young scamp's ear, and yell, "Don't do that, Sammy!"

Fortunately, the grocery clerk, who had two boys of his own, knew a better way to handle the situation.

"Sammy," he called to the boy. "Do you go to school?"

"Sure!"

"Well, let's see how smart you are. How many reasons can you think of for not climbing on those potatoes?"

Sammy got down off the potatoes, spread his feet apart, put his hands in his pockets, knit his brow, and thought hard.

" 'Cause Mom don't want me to," he blurted out.

"Why?"

" 'Cause I'll get dirty."

"Oh, come on, Sammy, you got to think better than that!"

Right away Sammy's ingenious little mind began to think of other reasons.

" 'Cause it might hurt the potatoes, and 'cause it makes me dirty, and 'cause you and Mommy don't want me to, and 'cause I might kick some one, and 'cause I might fall off the potatoes, and 'cause—well, them potatoes is heavy, ain't they? And if they'd fall on ya, they'd kill ya."

"Now you've got it, Sammy. You know, you're a smart boy. It's because the potatoes might fall on YOU and hurt you."

This Philadelphia grocery clerk was wise. In the first place, he didn't use the "don't do that, Sammy" possible solution to the problem which is so overused by parents, but which seldom works. If you have any doubt at all on this point, the next time you are in the presence of children with their fathers or mothers, count the number of times the parents say, "Don't do that."

They're like the Irish woman with the mischievous boy who was always getting into trouble. "Agnes," she yelled to her daughter, "go and find out what Jackie's doing and tell him to quit."

Naturally, children busy themselves with a lot of things that they shouldn't be doing, and it is a parent's frequent task to get them to stop. But "Don't do that" becomes so commonplace that the child no longer hears it. The real problem is two-fold. First, to get the child's attention, because, as we all know, children are usually preoccupied. And second, to get the child to understand *why* he is to discontinue doing something which is obviously interesting to him, or he wouldn't be doing it.

When you ask a child a question, and he gives you any answer, you can at least be sure that you have his attention. And if you can get the child to think long enough to hit on a *good* reason for not doing something, then you can be certain that he understands *why* he should not do it, in terms of a reason that makes sense to him, or he would never have thought of it.

Next time one of your children does something or wants to do something he shouldn't, just try this "can you think of any good reasons why you shouldn't?" approach, and you'll be surprised at how well it works out. In fact, it usually leads to discussion and your child comes out of it with some real understanding.

We've used this method a lot in our home. And if one of

the children balks and can't think of anything, we simply say, "Well, go to your room and think it over and don't come out until you *have* thought of some good reasons." It doesn't take them very long to re-appear.

PROMOTE A FREE EXCHANGE OF IDEAS WITH YOUR CHILDREN

The second way to reduce emergencies and conflicts with your children is to spend plenty of time with them in wide-open discussions of all kinds of subjects *before* emergencies and conflicts arise so that they get plenty of practice in a free and democratic exchange of ideas with you.

It's not enough for parents to be *right* about things. Every possible effort should be made to arrive at a common agreement among *all* members of the family, including the children, on what is right and what is wrong in all kinds of situations, *before* emergencies arise, so that when they *do* arise, the children know how to act.

For example, after-dinner discussion is an established institution at our house. It is understood by everyone in the family that that's the time to bring up any important questions which need to be thoroughly threshed out. Anyone may bring up any subject he wishes—lipstick, Latin, boys, homework, power politics, Egyptology, girls, baseball, vacation, chewing gum, United Nations, clothes, etiquette, music lessons, neighbors, dogs, race prejudice, swimming, babies, atomic bombs, smoking, dates, careers, drinking, movies, petting, dancing, human relations, bedtime rules, airplanes. I don't know what it will be tonight. Last night it was religion.

With no restrictions on subject matter, it is only natural that every now and then a child says something that, at first, leads one to believe that he is headed straight for the bad place in a berry basket. But we have gradually developed the habit of not being surprised, no matter what the children say. This, I think, is the first and the most important reason why our after-dinner discussions are so helpful. I've learned many of the facts of life from our children, and if any of them is the least bit hesitant about letting me know exactly what he thinks on any subject, I haven't noticed it.

The second reason why our family forum works is that we have developed the habit of saying "Yes" to any unimportant proposal, and not saying "Yes" or "No" to any important proposal—until it has been fully discussed and explored. This simple separation of what's important from what isn't cuts down the petty arguments that make mountains out of mole-hills.

If the problem at hand is really important, however, we take plenty of time to make up our minds.

And that brings up the third reason why our daily discussions are so popular. When a vote is taken on any question whatsoever, each of the children casts a vote which weighs just as much as does their mother's or mine. And it's surprising how conservative children are when, after full consideration of all the pros and cons, they are given the responsibility of casting their own votes.

Every now and then a ticklish subject comes up. But what better place is there to discuss ticklish subjects than at home? Although parents may feel that smoking and drinking and petting are dangerous, those who tell their adolescent son that "smoking will stunt your growth," and "a drink leads to destruction," or those who try to frighten their adolescent daughter by warning that "a kiss leads to ruin," are certain to suffer the dwindling confidence of their children. Children don't believe parents who talk like that, because what their parents tell them does not agree with what they learn from more authoritative sources and see with their own eyes.

It isn't necessary to depend on incredible statements to persuade a child to live as he should. There are always plenty of good reasons for his doing so.

It is better for parents to spend their time pointing out the truth, the need for judgment, the need for control, how to think, what to do and what to say to keep things from getting out of hand, and why such precautions make sense, than it is for them to get excited and try to shock their children into doing what's right.

Whether you run your own family forum or not, if you can gradually develop the habit of not being shocked or surprised at what your children say or what your children do, they will be more likely to tell you the truth about what they think and what they do. If you can develop the habit of granting all their less important requests, if you can develop the habit of the delayed response instead of a quick and arbitrary decision when important matters come up, if you will adopt the old democratic voting principle and give each child the feeling of dignity and responsibility which goes with the casting of his own vote, you will begin to have a perfectly free exchange of ideas in your home.

It is this free exchange of ideas between parent and child that makes your counsel eagerly sought and willingly followed when your child needs a counselor most. And it is this free exchange of ideas that makes it easy for you to arrive at common agreements with your children on what is right and what is wrong.

For instance, children are always asking for money for something or other, so we have arrived at a common agreement with ours that they will have a chance to *earn* the money they would like to have by helping out around the house and having a real part in keeping things in order. Consequently, they have learned to stop pestering us for money all the time. They know that the way to get the money they want is to keep on the lookout for things to do.

In our family forum, we discuss and agree upon all kinds of rules and regulations designed to help us to live peacefully together and respect each other's rights and property and feelings. We agree on fines and penalties to be imposed on anyone who violates these rules and regulations.

If my boy swears, it costs him a nickel. If I swear, it costs me a nickel. We've agreed on the fairness of that. If two of the children get into a quarrel, and one swings on the other, it costs the swinger a dime. We've agreed on the fairness of that. If two of the children involve themselves in a heated argument, and do not calm down when they are asked to, they both go on "silence" for five minutes, which provides a cooling-off period. We've agreed on that. And so on.

We've agreed on all these things in our *calmer* moments, in our periodic discussions, which are held for the specific purpose of arriving at common agreements about anything that has to do with living together and working together sensibly and peacefully.

Under those circumstances, when one violates a rule that has been commonly agreed on, he expects to pay the penalty that has been commonly agreed upon. And he does so willingly because he's had a part in setting up all rules and penalties.

Children, like grownups, want a sense of security. They want to know the rules of the game. Once they know the rules, once they know that the rules make sense, once they have the satisfaction of having a part in making the rules, they abide by them willingly. And in the exceptional instance, when they forget, or lose control, and violate the rules, they are perfectly willing to pay whatever penalty they have agreed upon in their calmer moments. After all, we are all outlaws to some extent. We all have our "outlaw" moments.

Whenever they violate a rule, they are dealt with tolerantly. We try to understand why it happened. We help them to be right. We use our previous agreement as the basis for persuading them to try not to let it happen again.

Under these conditions, we rarely, very rarely, are obliged to consider the use of force in our home.

But the significant thing is this. *The enforcement agency is always present.* If it ever came to a showdown, we've "got what it takes" to force any one of our children to abide by the rules and regulations they have agreed upon and to respect the rights of others.

So it becomes apparent that although the intelligent use of force is preceded, whenever possible, by persuasion— common agreements on what's right and the full use of peaceful discussion—the presence of an enforcement agency that "has what it takes" is a necessary element if one is to be sure of keeping peace even in his own family.

CHAPTER IX

The Use of Force in Business and Industry

No matter what business, industry, art, trade, or profession you may be engaged in, you will immediately see that there are certain situations in which you might consider the use of force, but more in which you cannot.

No matter how right you are, no matter if you have perfectly applied all the principles having to do with the psychology of persuasion, if persuasion fails, you cannot force anyone to buy your products or your services, for the simple reason that "you haven't got what it takes" to compel anyone to patronize you. However, if someone refuses to pay you for goods delivered or services rendered, or if he violates any other kind of valid business contract, you may have to consider the use of force through the courts.

In any of your personal relations with an employer, you may be right and you may have exhausted all known means of persuasion. But it may be dangerous for you to assume that you've "got what it takes" to force your employer to do what you want him to do.

Whenever I hear a man say, "Why . . . I've got them just where I want them. If I ever left them, everything would be in a mess. They *can't* get along without me," my answer is always "Take my word for it . . . they *can!*"

And in all your relations with fellow workers, the use of

force *can* be disastrous. Any person who tries to fight his way to success in any organization by trampling on others, or by using any kind of "power play," sooner or later finds that he has forced himself out of the picture. And when he "hits the skids," he meets the same people on the way down as he met going up. Naturally, instead of breaking his fall, these people help him to fall further.

Meanwhile, as we all know, force is commonly used, and misused, in business and industry, and it is important indeed for those who have any kind of power over others at their command to understand thoroughly the conditions which must precede the safe and proper use of that power.

THE POWER TO CALL A STRIKE

One of the commonest uses of force in industry is that which is employed by a union leader when he calls a strike.

The main reason why unions exist is that the members of these unions feel that they must bargain collectively with employers in order to secure the wages and the working conditions and the other benefits they think they are entitled to, and that they must be in a strong economic position to enforce their demands with a strike, if necessary.

Sometimes, the power to call a strike is misused by union leaders. Union leaders, like the leaders in any other field, do not always use their power intelligently.

But you will find that the quality of leadership in any particular union is usually a reflection of the conditions which that union has to meet. If a union is being forced to fight for its very existence, you may expect to find a leader who is difficult to work with. But when a union has earned an accepted place in the structure of any company or industry, you are more likely to find a leader who is able and reasonable.

In fact, my observations of union leaders bring me to the

conclusion that a man needs just about the same qualities and abilities to become a successful union leader as he needs to become a successful leader in any other field. Certainly, any union leader's cause must be just and he must be talented in the science of peaceful persuasion if he is truly to serve those who follow him.

Any union, of course, may succeed, temporarily, in forcing wages or other benefits beyond the economic ability of an employer or an industry to pay. But under these circumstances, the employer or the industry suffers in competition with other employers and industries, sooner or later workers have to be laid off, and the result is detrimental to the union itself. After all, no enlightened union leader is interested in defeating his own purposes.

Union leaders who serve their organizations best are those who realize that, before they can even consider the possibility of calling a strike, their demands must be fair, they must make every possible effort to arrive at a peaceful agreement with employers, and they must be in a strong economic position if they are to have what it takes to enforce their demands.

Within my own experience, I have seen several cases in which a union representative, in the heat of argument, threatened a strike, only to find out later that he did not enjoy the support of the head of his union—because he wasn't right, or because he showed an unwillingness to submit his grievance to quiet deliberation.

One of the ablest labor leaders in the nation recently told me, "You'll find that, with few exceptions, the labor leaders who finally get to the top and stay there are men who can see both sides of a dispute, men who are perfectly honest with their members and who aren't afraid to tell the members when their cause is wrong, men who avoid a strike like a plague. They know that any time they have to call a strike to get what they want, that's no great feather in their cap. The loss in wages, when a strike is called, may eat up all the gains you get, even if you win."

THE POWER TO HIRE AND TO FIRE

Business and industrial supervisors and executives who have the power to hire and to fire must also use that power with care if they are to achieve desirable results.

When an employee is hired, both the employer and the employee are usually in a happy frame of mind. But when an employee is fired, that's an expensive and distasteful experience for everyone concerned. And all too often it can be traced to one or both of two mistakes: (1) the employee never should have been hired in the first place, and/or (2) the employee was not properly trained.

No matter where you go, you'll find agreement that one of the most important continuing duties of management is to select and to train the right kind of manpower for the intelligent operation, direction, and extension of its business, and that any company which fails to do this is headed for failure and ultimate extinction.

Meanwhile, some sound methods for selection and training have been developed and a few leading organizations have put these methods to work. But for the most part, we find more emphasis on talk than on application. And much of the application falls short of sound business practice.

It is still far more common than it is unique for an employer to select the candidate for an important job who "talks the best job" or "clicks" in the first interview, and to blind himself to the fact that the fellow who makes the best first impression in a personal interview often turns out to be weak in actual performance. It's easy for us to be overimpressed by some "brilliant" candidate, only to find out later that this master mind has an amazing facility for antagonizing everyone else in the organization.

Every time I analyze a batch of "exit interviews," I am reminded all over again that the failure of an employee is seldom due to his lack of ability. An analysis I just completed showed that 84 per cent of these failures could be attributed to faulty human relations resulting in an insufficient desire to work at the job. And this is typical.

Yet, in selecting employees, industry still puts primary emphasis on *ability*. Even those who have developed elaborate pretesting procedures employ tests which, for the most part, reveal a person's ability to fill the job at hand.

True, a few scattered attempts have been made, in recent years, to pretest a candidate's facility in human relations. But rarely is any attempt made to discover, in advance of employment, whether or not a candidate's *inner desires* are in harmony with what he can accomplish in the job at hand.

In most business organizations, formal employee orientation and training plans are not to be found. Even in those organizations which pride themselves on being most advanced, the training program is usually confined to the development of required abilities and does not include the training and development of required desires and human relations.

In looking into office and factory operations, I am often amazed at the little attention a new employee gets after he's told what to do and where to work. Apparently, it has not yet dawned on most supervisors that unless a person is treated like a human being instead of part of a machine, unless he is reasonably happy in his job, unless he is made to feel that he plays an important part in the business, we are likely to find that worker "just going through the motions." And we are likely to wind up with a lot of problem cases.

The important point to remember is that orientation and training begin on the very first day on the job—whether a definite program exists or not. If a worker is merely hired, taken to his supervisor, and forgotten, he is still being trained. He is being trained negatively by default. Most workers start out with a natural desire to succeed on any job they undertake. But if they are ignored most of the time, and simply ordered around the rest of the time, it doesn't take very long for them to "seek the level of their group" and lose whatever desire they might have started with to "make good."

There's no good reason why a new employee shouldn't be given a reasonably complete statement about his company and the advantages of working there on his very first day on the job. This is often forgotten.

As one executive told me, "This is a good place to work. It's steady. We pay good wages, pay for holidays and vacations, give frequent raises and promotions. Whenever anyone's sick, he gets his regular wages just the same. Trouble is, we keep most of these things a secret, and it takes a new employee a year to find out that this is a good place to work."

Much of this kind of information can be put into a simple booklet welcoming new employees.

Sometimes it is possible to take even the routine line worker on a quick tour of the office or the plant before he is taken to his immediate supervisor. This is not only a courtesy but a compliment. It helps the newcomer to see the importance of his job—how it is related to the entire operation.

When the new employee is introduced to his immediate supervisor who, in turn, introduces him to his immediate co-workers, one of his co-workers is sometimes appointed "angel" to answer minor personal questions and to see that the newcomer quickly feels at home in the group.

How the supervisor handles the new employee probably has more to do with the development of his desire to work on the job than any other single factor in the entire work environment. If the supervisor trains the worker in such a way that the worker likes him personally and looks to him for leadership, you can be pretty sure the worker will continue to desire to work at his job.

Furthermore, training should be looked upon as a continuing program. It isn't enough just to give the new employee a proper welcome, some initial training, and let it go at that. The long-range fate of every employee is largely in the hands of his immediate supervisor whose job is to follow through on every order; to compliment a man on work well done; to offer suggestions and corrections when work is poorly done; and to prove by his actions, day in and day out, that he is interested in the welfare and in the progress of everyone under his supervision.

Careful selection and training will do more than anything I know of to improve morale and to reduce expensive mistakes in hiring and firing. But no matter how carefully we perform these tasks, we may always have a few problem cases.

WHAT TO DO ABOUT PROBLEM PERSONNEL

Every able executive knows that before he fires anyone, he must be right, right in the employee's eyes as well as his own, and second, he must have exercised a reasonable amount of tolerance and persuasion before he forces anyone to leave his employ if he is to enjoy and sustain the good will of his other employees which is so necessary to the conduct of any business enterprise. No company can afford to have a flock of enemies among its former employees.

However, even those business executives who are absolutely fair, and who depend primarily on peaceful persuasion in all their contacts with those who work for them, know that every now and then occasions do arise when they are obliged to use force against those who are unfair to their company or who are unfit for their jobs.

Take, for example, the accountant who was always pestering his boss for a chance to get on the sales staff. Finally it was agreed that he would join the sales staff "on trial," and that if he did not make good within a reasonable length of time, he would return to the accounting department.

He failed as a salesman. When the sales manager suggested that he return to the accounting department, this young man expressed his unwillingness to do so, and in spite of all the sales manager's efforts to persuade him, the young man seemed unconvinced, continuing to alibi his failure as a salesman and maintaining that he deserved still another chance.

Finally, the sales manager had to force his transfer.

At first, this young man thought he had been given a dirty deal. But two years after he had returned to the accounting department, made some progress, and realized that he really belonged there, his mind re-opened to the sales manager who had put him there, and today he feels grateful to this sales executive for forcing him, for his own good, into the kind of work he was best fitted for.

This sales executive uses a lot of persuasion. But when he's right, and when persuasion fails, he never hesitates to use force whenever it's in the best interests of his company and his men.

Before he hires a man, he makes the conditions of employment perfectly clear and arrives at an agreement with the new man that is perfectly fair and square.

When a man makes a mistake, he reasons with him. I heard him say to one salesman who pulled a boner, "Well, Joe, that's excusable. We all make mistakes. But let's try not to make *that* one again."

When this man made the same mistake the second time, this executive's attitude was, "Joe, this has happened before. You know, we can't afford to have our men continue to make the same mistakes over and over again. It's not fair to the business. After all, we *are* running a business—a highly competitive business. If we were to permit our men to continue to make the same mistakes over and over again, Joe, it wouldn't be long until we wouldn't have a business.

"There are a great many things I like about you, Joe, and I don't want to be forced to let you go. It wouldn't be fair to you for me to encourage you in any careless habits, and it wouldn't be fair to the rest of the people in this business or to the people we serve for me to permit you to go on like this. But if you continue to make this same mistake, you'll leave me no alternative. So let's say that you'll be given another chance. But this is the last one. Is that fair?"

I've seen this sales executive force the transfer or the resignation of a number of men, and yet I have never seen a case where the man who was transferred or fired didn't ultimately realize that he had it coming to him and that it was for his own good.

This executive is able, he's aggressive, he has one of the fastest moving sales forces in his industry. He pays top salaries to his men. He has a right to expect top performance.

His dealings with men represent an outstanding example of the intelligent use of force in business because he conforms to the fair and essential conditions which should precede the use of force—he arrives at a common agreement with his men concerning what's right and what's wrong; even when a man makes a mistake, he helps that man to correct it through persuasion; and only after a man continues doing something wrong time after time will this executive force him out.

However, as we all know, many supervisors and executives are not so highly skilled in handling problem cases. It is so easy to get mad and fire a person who creates organizational problems, but it is more economical, more considerate, and more intelligent to reason with the person, show him the error of his ways, and save the high cost of training someone to replace him.

For example, not long ago the production director of a large plant told me that he was going to have to fire Ben

Irwin, one of his assistant engineers, "because Ben insults everyone around here."

When I went into Ben's office to have a chat with him, he complained bitterly about the company in general and "everyone who works around here."

"You're the first one who's been in here today who hasn't argued with me. I seem to annoy everyone. Sometimes I wonder why I work in such a lousy place."

"Well, the only reason I haven't argued with you," I told him, "is that I came into your office *expecting* to be insulted, and I decided in advance that I wouldn't let it upset me. You see, Ben, there are three elements of success in any job: first, our *desire* to work at the job; second, our *ability* to do the job; and third, our capacity for *getting along with the people* we work with.

"The trouble is, most people just fly on one motor. There are plenty of people who hold their jobs for one reason alone —their outstanding ability. The more ability a man has, the less he 'needs' people, and the weaker he's likely to be in his human relations. On the other hand, if a fellow hasn't got a brain, he's just got to be nice to people—strong in his human relations.

"You're a great engineer, Ben. You have creative ability. You know a lot about automatic machinery. You're ingenious in solving problems in design. You're valuable to this company. But you're certainly no master in human relations.

"I believe you'd have a great future with this company if you could get along a little better with the fellows you work with. And I think this would do more than anything else in the world to make you like your job better. You'd enjoy it more. You're flying on one motor, Ben. If you can get the other two working, your future's assured. If you don't, you'll find it tough going no matter where you work."

It was apparent that the importance of good human relations had never dawned on Ben. Up to that time, he thought, "All you have to do is to be right, and if anyone doesn't like it, let him lump it."

Now, Ben's smart. As soon as he realized other people could do a lot to speed or to retard his progress, he began smiling more and snarling less.

Almost overnight, he stopped ignoring and insulting people. Even his wife told the chief engineer, "Something's happened to Ben. He's not nearly so jumpy as he used to be."

Today, Ben has a good chance of becoming the next chief engineer.

I didn't want to see Ben fired, because it would have cost the company several thousand dollars to find another engineer as good as Ben and it probably would have resulted in some expensive delays in production.

In another company, an office manager was all ready to fire the chief file clerk and librarian. "She's got B.O.," he told me. "And every girl who works in there complains."

"Who's her best friend among the girls?" I asked.

The general manager's secretary had known her for years. She had a "personal talk" with the librarian; the B.O. disappeared.

It would have cost this company nine hundred dollars to train a new chief file clerk and librarian.

In still another company, the president and general manager told me, "We ought to get rid of Joe Harris in Detroit. Joe's drunk half the time . . . only works a couple of hours a day."

"May I see Harris's sales record?" I asked.

Joe's sales record showed that, while he wasn't the top man on the staff, his sales were well above the average.

"I think maybe we can learn something from this man," I told the sales chief.

"How do you mean?"

"Well, if Joe only works a couple of hours a day and he still turns in a sales record like this, he may know more about selling than any of us."

A week later, in Detroit, I spent a few days with Joe Harris—and enjoyed myself immensely. He *was* a late starter in the morning! It was usually around 10:30 in the morning before we actually faced a prospect. He always took plenty of time to eat lunch in grand style. And around 3:30 he was ready to repair to a downtown bar for refreshments.

But on the relatively few sales calls he did make, he was terrific. As I observed him, it seemed to me he had a sales procedure that might well be followed by many another salesman on the staff. His sales per call were unusually high.

"They're shooting at you in the home office, Joe," I told him. "They say you're drunk half the time . . . only work a couple of hours a day. They're even thinking of letting you out. But when I looked at your sales record, I knew you were a great salesman . . . maybe the greatest the company's got. Why don't you fool 'em, Joe? If you worked three hours a day instead of two hours a day, you'd be top man."

That was enough.

Within three months, Joe led the sales staff. A short time later, he went on the wagon. Within two years, I recommended him for a division manager's job, which he got.

If Joe had been fired, we'd have lost one of the best men we had, and it would have cost the company $3,600 to hire and to train a new man for Detroit.

It's a disagreeable job, at best, to fire anyone. It should be done only as a last resort.

Obviously, it took more time to solve these cases than it does to tell about them. And many other cases do not solve so easily. But when we stop to realize what we've got to gain by solving a problem case, we can see it justifies considerable thought and attention.

If we only stopped to realize that no one is perfect, we'd think twice before we fired the problem case. Often we fire one person who has something wrong with him, then we turn around and hire someone else, and it takes us a year to find out what's wrong with him. If we spent our time improving and building the people we have, we'd be further along and money ahead.

Another thing, whether you're the president, a chief executive, a department head, or just a supervisor in your company, you don't build any character or prestige for yourself by firing people. But you do by building them. Anyone will tell you that the boss who holds his workers together can't help succeed, while the one who doesn't is viewed with suspicion.

Sometimes you run into a case of a person who isn't doing a good job because he's miscast.

One man who was working on a tooth-paste packing line was close to the snapping point. He was a "troublemaker." I picked him up on an "exit interview." When I learned woodworking was his hobby, that he had a shop in his basement, and that he yearned to be a craftsman, I had him transferred to the job of carpenter's helper in the plant shop. This gave him a chance to exercise his latent creativeness, and he thanks me every time we meet.

Sometimes you'll find a worker who just doesn't belong in any department of your business. After all, no business is big enough or has sufficient variety of occupations to satisfy everyone's career desires.

If you're convinced a person would be better off working some place else, the best thing to do is to have a heart-to-heart talk with him and tell him so. Then help him to get relocated where he belongs—where he'll do better and where he'll be happier in the long run. He'll thank you and your company for that kind of help.

To summarize, you can gradually reduce the number of problem cases in your organization by improving your methods for the selection of new employees.

You can reduce your number of problem cases by introducing a plan for orientation and training which prevents good workers from deteriorating into problem cases *after* they are employed.

Finally, the thoughtful handling of the problem case with a view to (1) correcting his faults and building him up in his present job, (2) transferring him to a more suitable job within the organization, or (3) as a last resort, helping him to get into another company where he'll be happier and of greater service . . . this kind of treatment of the problem case will reduce expensive mistakes, build personal prestige for you, and create lasting good will for your organization.

C H A P T E R   X

The Use of Force in Government

The United States of America is a peace-loving nation and the American way of life is looked upon as a model in other parts of the world. But even the American citizens with whom you associate in your own community, state, and nation have not yet achieved such a high and uniform degree of civilization that we are ready to dispense with law enforcement agencies.

FORCE IN THE COMMUNITY, STATE, AND NATION

Law enforcement agencies in the community, state, and nation—all the way from the local police force to the FBI and other agencies of the Federal government—have a commonly recognized, accepted, and approved place in keeping the peace and in protecting us against the outlaw in our midst. For there always have been outlaws among us and there probably will continue to be for many centuries to come.

When these law enforcement agencies "have what it takes" to accomplish their purpose, their very presence discourages many with outlaw tendencies from ever becoming dangerous outlaws.

But as we know, this is only one of the requirements for the intelligent use of force.

We are already familiar with the other two conditions which must attend the intelligent use of force.

First, the laws—local, state, or national—which are enforced by the law enforcement agencies, must be right. They must represent rules and regulations which are acceptable to the vast majority of the population called upon to abide by them. And in a democracy there are peaceful procedures for discontinuing any law, rule, or regulation which does not meet this fundamental requirement.

Whenever a law does not enjoy popular support, it becomes difficult to enforce and, in extreme cases, there just isn't enough force in our normal law enforcement agencies to make such a law stick.

The prohibition amendment was a notable example of this. There were so many people violating the law that it would have been necessary to have a prohibitive number of policemen to enforce it. In addition, because the law did not make sense to such a high percentage of our citizens, it led to the formation of innumerable illegal rackets which were directly or indirectly patronized and supported by a large percentage of the people.

The use of what force they had was reluctantly employed by many of the law enforcement officers themselves, and many of these officers became enmeshed in illegal rackets for the simple reason that the law was not *just* in so many people's eyes, and this vital condition for the intelligent use of force was therefore absent.

It seldom takes more than a limited number of enforcement officers to enforce a law that is just. Because the vast majority of people are in sympathy with it, outlaws are exceptional, and the enforcement officer has his heart in the work.

As far as the other requirement for the intelligent use of force is concerned—that it should be preceded by all reasonable means for peaceful discussion and persuasion—we know that the courts, whether local, state, or national, are set up to give everyone a fair trial. They must temper justice with mercy and they must utilize moderate fines and other forms of warnings and persuasion before they resort to imprisonment.

An interesting example of this occurred not long ago in a small town in Connecticut, where two teen-agers appeared before the Town Court Judge, Paul MacDonald, charged with engaging in a fist fight back of the town hall.

Instead of fining these young men or sending them to jail for disorderly conduct, Judge MacDonald came up with a constructive penalty that was wise indeed. He ordered the young men to write two essays: one on "Good Government" and the other on "Why Disorderly Conduct Should Not Be Tolerated."

The youths came through creditably with worth-while papers on these subjects and the judge directed that the cases be stricken from the court records so that the boys would have no police records against them in future life.

Both of the young men felt that their punishment was just and proper and made them think.

Even in the case of major crimes, the first offender is usually treated more leniently than the second or the third, if the courts are to receive the whole-hearted respect and approval of the public at large.

Whenever an exceptional instance arises, in which a court of justice shows that it is unworthy of the name, sooner or later it loses its prestige, becomes the subject of investigation, and the person or persons responsible for its misuse of force are removed.

Within the experience of most of us, we know of at least one or two such instances. Most people are in sympathy with sensible speed laws, for example, but whenever some short-sighted local law enforcement agency deliberately sets up a speed trap and proceeds to slap unreasonable fines on first offenders, this nasty situation becomes the subject of a sufficient number of protests to result in the elimination of such unjustified and unintelligent use of force.

So that even our courts cannot safely engage in the use of force without just laws and without a reasonable amount of discussion and persuasion. Still, force will always have its place as the third essential element in dealing with the confirmed outlaw.

FORCE IN INTERNATIONAL RELATIONS

If force has an essential place in preserving peace in our home, in our business, in our community, in our state, and in our nation, what right has anyone to expect that force should not occupy an important place in our international relations? And what right has anyone to expect that we can ever achieve world peace unless, and until, we have an international police force that "has what it takes?"

Ever since the Peloponnesians warred against Athens, 431 years before the birth of Christ, nearly every war in the history of the world has been advertised as the war that would end wars and lead to a permanent peace. And at the conclusion of each of these wars, the more peace-loving nations have laid away their instruments of force and entered into an era of complacency which assumed that, from then on, nations could be relied upon to settle all their disputes by peaceful negotiations.

Yet, out of the 3,521 years of human history recorded up to date, there have been only 268 years of peace! So that it may be astonishing, but it is nonetheless true, that international warfare is typical rather than unique.

One thing is certain. If and when peace among all the nations of the earth is maintained, it will be accomplished in the very same way and with the use of the very same fundamental implements of peace that we use in our own home, in our own business, in our own community, in our own state, and in our own nation.

In other words, peaceful relations among nations must rest on:

1. Common agreements concerning what is right and what is wrong.
2. The use of all reasonable means for peaceful discussion and persuasion.
3. The maintenance of an international police force that "has what it takes" to enforce international agreements.

The League of Nations, set up after World War I, represented an incomplete and unsuccessful step in this direction.

It did some good work. It condemned Japanese aggression in Manchuria, Italian aggression in Ethiopia, and expelled Russia for its invasion of Finland. But the United States never joined the League. In 1933, Germany and Japan resigned, followed by the resignations of Guatemala, Honduras, and Nicaragua in 1936. The League never had "what it takes" to enforce its decisions, and in July, 1940, it was disbanded.

The present hope is that all three of the conditions given above will be realized within the framework of the United Nations.

Right now we have, at least on paper, in the Charter of the United Nations, a general agreement among the vast majority of all the nations of the earth concerning what's right and what's wrong.

Here is the preamble of that Charter:

WE, the peoples of the United Nations determined to save succeeding generations from the scourge of war, which twice in our lifeti ne has brought untold sorrow to mankind, and

To reaffirm faith in fundamental human rights, in the dignity and worth of the human person, in the equal rights of men and women and of nations large and small, and

To establish conditions under which justice and respect for the obligations arising from treaties and other sources of international law can be maintained, and

To promote social progress and better standards of life in larger freedom, and for these ends

To practice tolerance and live together in peace with one another as good neighbors, and

To unite our strength to maintain international peace and security, and

To insure, by the acceptance of principles and the institution of methods, that armed force shall not be used, save in the common interest, and

To employ international machinery for the promotion of the economic and social advancement of all peoples, have resolved to combine our efforts to accomplish these aims.

Accordingly, our respective governments, through representatives assembled in the city of San Francisco, who have exhibited their full powers found to be in good and due form, have agreed to the present Charter of the United Nations and do hereby establish an international organization to be known as the United Nations.

Those who take the time to read the Charter of the United Nations, in its entirety, will find that there is adequate provision within the organization of the United Nations for peaceful discussion of differences, which represents the second main requirement for international peace.

But when we come to the third main requirement—the maintenance of an international police force that "has what it takes" to enforce the aims of the United Nations, if necessary—there is still much to be done.

It isn't an easy matter to maintain a police force strong enough to assure international peace when some of the leading nations of the world do not *practice* freedom and democracy within their own borders, and continue to follow an international policy of aggression which is contrary to the fundamental aims of the United Nations.

The main trouble is that so many of the peoples of the earth have had so little experience in self-government that they have no adequate understanding of a truly democratic way of life, and, as long as they are ruled by dictators, they have little chance to gain the required experience.

It's a big job, but we must do everything in our power (1) to awaken the *desire* for freedom and self-government in the minds and hearts of those who are under a dictatorial form of government, and (2) to encourage the development of the right kind of *leadership* in these countries so that the people will be able to choose representatives who reflect the real spirit of democracy.

Meanwhile, as we work for these ends, there is no room for either over-optimism or utter despair. The important thing is that we fully understand the huge dimensions of the task while we patiently engage in an all-out effort gradually to achieve the primary conditions for international peace. Obviously, all these favorable conditions cannot be secured overnight. But they can gradually be realized down through the years.

Our progress along these lines can be speeded up enormously if we will just try to understand the people who live in totalitarian countries and learn how to talk their language. And we will be better able to talk the language of the masses in nations still ruled by dictators if we study the history of these nations, understand the full significance of the fact that these people have never had any real experience in self-government, and realize that these people must gradually learn how to govern themselves.

We will make little or no headway in converting the followers of communism or any other form of totalitarianism merely by condemning them as "crackpots." We must show these people, by our own example, that the material and spiritual benefits of the democratic way of life are worth striving for, and we must let them know that we stand ready to help them in every way we can in their struggles for freedom.

This is the way in which we have been gradually winning nations, one at a time, to the democratic way of life, and if we keep working along these constructive lines, there is every reason to believe that, in due time, the majority of the people in all the leading nations of the world will finally understand and embrace the principles of freedom and democracy.

When this great step is achieved, it will be a lot easier for nations to resolve their differences and to arrive at sound decisions and agreements by peaceful persuasion—agreements which all leading nations wish to enforce—and under these conditions a relatively small international police force would be sufficient to enforce world order.

Until that time comes, however, the free nations of the world must not only try to convert totalitarian nations to a democratic system. They must also maintain enough power to overcome any attempt to conquer the democracies.

The year 1950 will go down in history because during this year, for the first time in the history of man, the nations of the world, formally organized within the United Nations, voted to use the power of an international police force to fight aggression in Korea.

As long as the balance of power is in the hands of the free world, there is a good chance that the totalitarian nations will not commit themselves to an all-out war which they could not win. But nations have blundered into wars before that they could not successfully finish, and there is no final assurance that it cannot happen again. Meanwhile, with the world as split as it is today, the cost of maintaining a force strong enough to protect its democratic way of life will continue high, and, in the last analysis, it can be safely reduced only as leading totalitarian nations are converted to democracy.

As we work for peace, let's not be discouraged by those who are already saying that the United Nations "is a failure because it has not prevented aggression." There are many impatient people who do not seem to understand the huge dimensions of the task of achieving the fundamental conditions for international peace. The stronger we make the United Nations, the less chance there will be of any potential aggressor challenging that strength.

Don't let a bunch of stuffed shirts get you all mixed up with a lot of highfalutin' language and short-sighted arguments about international relations and international peace. When we look at nations in terms of individuals, the complicated and obscure problems in international relations have a way of simplifying and clarifying themselves.

Whenever you have a problem in international relations to figure out, just go back to the simple fundamental laws of human relations that apply right in your own home— and you can't go wrong.

The secret of the oceans is in each tiny atom of water. And the fundamental laws of human relations are to be found operating in the smallest unit of human society—the family

The same elemental laws, the same essential conditions that work for peaceful living in your own family, also apply in a family of nations.

CHAPTER XI

The Universal Application of The Principles of Successful Human Relations

The laws of human relations are the very same the world over.

Once you've opened a person's mind by "putting yourself in his place" and "helping him to be right," you are certain to win his confidence if you show him that you are thinking in terms of his interests as well as your own, and that you are eager to serve his interests. That's the kind of evidence that gains anyone's confidence.

And if, in every new situation that arises, you continue to show your willingness to serve his interests, as well as your own, you will ultimately inspire his belief.

As we have seen, mutual confidence and belief are the only hope for civilized and productive relations among ourselves, our families, our friends, and among nations, races, creeds, or groups of any kind.

Confidence and belief are the very cornerstones of human society. Wherever confidence fails, civilization crumbles.

In most cases, it is possible to open the other fellow's mind, win his confidence, and inspire his belief, by persuasion.

But, as we have seen, the intelligent use of force still has a place, along with persuasion, in a world that has not yet come of age.

Whenever you encounter an exceptionally stubborn person, or group of persons, refusing to respond to persuasion, no matter what you do, you are automatically obliged to retire, surrender, or use force.

And before you elect to use force, whether you are dealing with an individual or a group, at home or abroad, you had better "be right"—not in your own eyes alone but in view of the common good; you had better "use all reasonable means for peaceful discussion and persuasion"; and you had better "have what it takes" to *force* the other fellow to do what's right for his own good and for the good of all concerned.

But remember that force, at best, is dynamite. And even after all hope of persuasion seems lost, always remember that the weak must continue to be patient and the strong can well afford to be.

No disease is ever controlled until we discover the responsible germ and find a method for destroying it. The germ that causes conflict is the closed mind. Individual warfare is merely the clash of two diseased closed minds. It is the closed mind that causes the little petty wars within our family, our business, and our intimate social groups—little personal wars that are just as contemptible, just as vicious, and even more destructive of our mental and moral fiber, because they are so often carried on with a deceitful smile and have none of the qualities of heroism which mark open warfare. And mass warfare is merely the spread of this mental disease among many individuals.

We cannot reduce either individual or mass conflict until we find out how to open the closed minds of the individuals who engage in conflict.

In this book, we have undertaken to expose this germ

that causes conflict, and to offer the simple mental attitude of helping the other fellow to be right, which is the one sure way to destroy the germ and pry open the closed mind.

This is the civilized mental attitude which not only straightens out your thinking in your personal relations with others but makes it virtually impossible for you to make vital mistakes in any of your human relations—a mental attitude so simple, so readily acceptable, and so easy to understand, that you will have no difficulty in using it immediately to make your everyday relations with others more pleasant and more productive.

This mental attitude conforms with all the fundamental rules for straight thinking; yet it relieves you of the technical complications of mastering and applying all these rules.

Those of you who consult the technical rules for straight thinking in the Appendix will readily see why this is so. You will see that there are four steps in orderly thinking: (1) observation, (2) definition of the problem, (3) the consideration of various possible solutions, and (4) the arriving at properly qualified conclusions. And it will become perfectly apparent to you that once you assume the simple mental attitude of helping the other fellow to be right, you automatically observe his point of view as well as your own, you open your mind to his problem as well as your own, you consider possible solutions that serve his interests as well as your own, and you arrive at mutually agreed-upon conclusions that serve the best interests of all concerned.

Obviously, there is no place for erroneous conclusion-jumping in a mind that is able to think straight, and when anyone assumes the mental attitude of helping the other fellow to be right, it is impossible for him to be prejudiced in any of his relations with individuals or groups of people.

We now know how to open closed minds, gain confidence, and inspire belief through the application of the fundamental principles of persuasion, and we now know the three basic conditions under which we may consider the use of force, if persuasion fails.

Now that we have defined the principles of successful human relations, however, the larger job still lies ahead— that of communicating these principles to others in such a way that the overwhelming majority of people throughout the world will thoroughly understand why it is wise to use these principles in the solution of their everyday human problems for their own good and for the good of all concerned.

Right now, there are some individuals, of course, who are able to see beyond their own selfish and short-sighted interests in the home; some employees who are willing to serve a business as a whole; some business executives and union leaders who appreciate the problems of management and labor and who understand the obligations of both to the general public; some citizens who can look beyond the horizons of their own community or state and act for the general good of their nation; and there are some men and women, in every nation in the world, who have enough breadth of vision to be able to see that they cannot be secure as long as the people in other nations suffer with poverty, disease, and miserable living standards, and that their own welfare is intimately and directly dependent upon the general welfare of *all* the nations of the world.

But we need more of such people. And one of the greatest challenges that education faces today throughout the world is to train more people to measure up to such standards.

I am unable to rid myself of the deep-rooted conviction that if we were to begin, even in grade school, to teach everyone the simple principles of human relations—just as we teach reading, writing, and arithmetic—it would soon have a profound effect on the world we live in.

For since nations, races, creeds, and groups of any kind are merely collections of individuals, as individuals all over the world become more civilized in their everyday relations with others, they will become more civilized in their larger mass relations.

Meanwhile, you do not have to wait until the world becomes more civilized before you begin to enjoy the benefits of acting more civilized yourself. In fact, you yourself can probably think of many instances in which you have already helped someone to be right and have enjoyed all the rewards. And your personal progress can be speeded up immediately by assuming this mental attitude in *more* of your everyday relations with others.

After all, it's a wonderful feeling to be in harmony with your environment—especially your human environment.

To be in tune with those around you, to help them to be right, fills you with a feeling of well-being and deep personal satisfaction.

Next time you feel mentally disturbed or upset about anything, just review in your mind what happened to cause this disturbance and you'll probably find that it's all because you're out of harmony with your human environment —you're helping someone to be wrong.

Then, just turn your mental attitude around and help that person to be right. Give him the benefit of every doubt and freely admit to yourself whatever mistakes you even *might* have made.

You'll feel better immediately and when you see that person you'll automatically say and do the right things because you feel right toward that person. You are in tune with him.

Yes, you can learn a lot about people and you can enjoy the warm affection of people if you'll just sit down and talk with them and help them to be right.

In fact, the moment you assume this mental attitude toward others, you find that it is easier for you to get along with others, easier for you to get their cooperation, easier for you to make all your relations with others more satisfying and more productive and more mutually profitable, easier for you to achieve your loftiest desires, easier for you to enjoy more peaceful relations with others at home and abroad.

So when you come right down to it, our job today is to help more people to be right in our everyday personal relations and to teach and to inspire others to do likewise.

Just try it and you'll find open minds and open hearts wherever you go.

APPENDIX

What is the National Institute For Straight Thinking?

So many readers of our previous books have written in asking, "What is The National Institute for Straight Thinking?" that we herewith make the answer to this question part and parcel of this book. The following facts on the background and present work of the Institute will help you to understand our purpose.

In 1922, while on the research staff at Carnegie Institute of Technology, Dr. William J. Reilly began some early attempts to adapt the organized thinking employed in the scientific laboratory to business and career problems.

Ten years later these experiments, started at Carnegie, culminated in the origination of twelve simple rules for straight thinking, and in the fall of 1932, Dr. Reilly founded the National Institute for Straight Thinking for the purpose of training men and women to use straight thinking in their business and career planning. Since that time, the rules have been successfully applied to a wide variety of other problems as well, and today the Institute offers counsel on business problems, career problems, and problems in the field of general education.

But let's go back.

135

AN IDEA IS BORN AT CARNEGIE

At Carnegie, Dr. Reilly observed the care and precision with which students in the scientific laboratory followed a certain approved procedure—how they tested their observations, defined their problems, gathered their evidence, and arrived at properly qualified conclusions. But he also noticed that when these same students stepped across the hall from the scientific laboratory to the study of problems in economics or business, they carried little of their orderly procedure with them, and seemed bewildered as to just how such problems should be handled.

Students in the laboratory were taught the scientific methods for analyzing the strength and the weakness of raw materials, in order to determine where these materials could best be used. But they were never taught any scientific methods for the study of their own basic abilities, likes, or dislikes, to find out in what field they could best be employed.

Intrigued by these obvious contradictions, Dr. Reilly began to adapt the scientific procedures of the laboratory to the two fields which interested him most—business and career planning.

In the field of business, he began by making a first-hand study of twenty of the nation's leading advertising agencies for the purpose of defining the primary functions of the modern advertising agency so that students of advertising could have a clearer understanding of this type of business organization.

In the career field, he began by asking engineering students at Carnegie why they were there. He found that apparently only a small percentage of these students had made a thoughtful selection of engineering as their lifework. For the most part, they had drifted into an engineering course for such reasons as: "they thought engineering was the coming thing," or "their family or friends suggested it," or "they had connections," or "there's good pay in it."

Tracing the history of those who had been graduated, he found that approximately two-thirds of the graduates wound up in lines of work other than engineering. All of which raised the question as to how many had been miscast at the outset in an engineering course.

As a result of these studies, Dr. Reilly began to work on a series of practical career tests which would help a young man to cast himself in the right role and make a more intelligent selection of his courses of study.

THE RULES FOR STRAIGHT THINKING ARE DEFINED

Later, while on the research staff at the University of Chicago where he received his Doctor's degree in philosophy, and at the University of Texas where he was associate professor of Business Administration and director of Market Studies, Dr. Reilly engaged in a comprehensive search of the literature on logic. This search revealed that, while orderly procedures had been followed for years in the pure sciences, yet apparently no one had ever defined the general process of straight thinking in the social sciences; no comprehensive rules had ever been set down to help the student to think straight on problems which involve human behavior.

Dr. Reilly then consulted with a number of outstanding educational leaders on the subject of straight thinking. Among them he found sympathetic agreement that "the whole idea of democratic education is to induce people to think, to think straight if possible, but to think always for themselves."

In all these consultations with logicians, psychologists, and social scientists, the orderly procedure followed in the scientific laboratory for years was used as the basis for the development of simple rules that could be applied safely to problems involving human behavior. Finally, twelve simple rules were defined and agreed upon.

RULES FOR STRAIGHT THINKING

I. RULES FOR MAKING PRECISE OBSERVATIONS

Rule 1. Define the primary facts in connection with your observation, and separate these facts from any opinions or impressions.

Rule 2. Analyze the facts, as far as they will permit, from the standpoint of what, when, where, and who.

II. RULES FOR DEFINING THE REAL PROBLEM AND CONSIDERING POSSIBLE SOLUTIONS

Rule 3. Construct a precise and analytical definition of the real problem from the standpoint of what, when, where, and who.

Rule 4. Keeping the total situation in mind, list all possible solutions that suggest themselves.

Rule 5. Classify these solutions in order of preference.

Rule 6. Select the most promising solutions for further examination.

III. RULES FOR SECURING EVIDENCE ON POSSIBLE SOLUTIONS

Rule 7. Expose yourself to sources of evidence on all sides of the question, rather than confine yourself to sources that give evidence only on one side.

Rule 8. Appraise the validity of your evidence from the standpoint of its source and the means used for gathering it.

Rule 9. Guard against the formation of opinions or premature judgments while in the process of examining evidence.

Rule 10. Keep the mind open and hospitable to new evidence on any side of the question.

IV. RULES FOR DRAWING CONCLUSIONS

Rule 11. Set up a balance sheet on each possible solution, stating your evidence for and against that course of action.

Rule 12. Weigh the relative importance of positive and negative evidence in each case, and draw your conclusion in favor of the best course (or courses) of action to be taken.

THE NATIONAL INSTITUTE FOR STRAIGHT THINKING IS FOUNDED

Soon after Dr. Reilly founded the National Institute for Straight Thinking, preliminary test work showed that those most interested in straight thinking are those who need it least—successful business leaders and outstanding young men who are open-mindedly reaching out in the direction of anything that will further improve their thinking and speed up their progress.

Consequently, the first Institute class in "Straight Thinking in Business" consisted of a seminar group of twelve leading business executives in New York—presidents, vice-presidents, and general managers. And the first Institute class in "Career Planning" consisted of a group of twelve "able young men in their thirties" who were suggested and recommended by these leading executives.

WHAT THE INSTITUTE IS DOING TODAY

Today the Institute continues to fulfill the purpose for which it was originally founded—to train business men and women to use straight thinking in their business and career planning.

In its business consultations, the Institute has been

called upon to guide the organization of new business enterprises, and to solve a wide variety of personnel, marketing, production, and organization problems for many of the largest manufacturers and industries in the United States.

In its career work, the Institute offers a private consultation program on career planning at the adult level, the college level, and the high-school level. Career counseling involves problems that are so personal and confidential that today the work of the Institute consists of individual consultations, rather than formal class work, with chief executives, able young men and women in their thirties, and exceptional younger men and women who come to the Institute for counsel. The Institute has developed, over a period of years, a series of practical career tests which reveal a person's basic abilities, and even more important, his personal like and dislike patterns. His basic strengths and weaknesses are measured in relation to his abilities, his desires, and his human relations. High-school and college students are counseled on their immediate educational programs, as well as their longer-range objectives. Adults are counseled on (1) the building of a salable background, (2) the development of personal sponsorship among potential buyers of their services, (3) the improvement of abilities, desire, and human relations, (4) the actual sale of personal services at the right price, and (5) the avocational search for some interest that promises to develop into one's own business beyond the age of fifty-five.

The Institute has recently undertaken the task of collaborating with high schools and colleges in the development and installation of courses of study in which the twelve rules for straight thinking are applied to (1) career planning and vocational guidance, (2) problems in human relations, and (3) business problems.

The Institute work enjoys the sponsorship of many leading executives and educators. Dr. Reilly's books on business planning, career planning, and human relations are now used in a number of high schools, colleges, and universities, and he has been engaged by such educational institutions to lecture on these important subjects.

The Institute work has been featured on all leading radio networks, the NBC television network, and the National Broadcasting Company has granted the Institute requested time for its "American Family Forum" Round-Table Discussions.

The work of the Institute has been featured in many leading national magazines, such as *Reader's Digest, Look, The American Magazine, Coronet, Pageant, The American Weekly, Parents' Magazine, American Business,* and *Your Life.*

From time to time, the Institute holds special educational events to which members are permitted to invite their friends.

INDEX